Lazzaro Spallanzani

Travels in the Two Sicilies

Vol. 1

Lazzaro Spallanzani

Travels in the Two Sicilies
Vol. 1

ISBN/EAN: 9783337346164

Printed in Europe, USA, Canada, Australia, Japan

Cover: Foto ©Andreas Hilbeck / pixelio.de

More available books at **www.hansebooks.com**

TRAVELS

IN THE

TWO SICILIES,

AND

SOME PARTS OF THE APENNINES.

Translated from the Original Italian of the

ABBE LAZZARO SPALLANZANI,

Professor-Royal of Natural History in the University of Pavia, and Superintendant of the Imperial Museum in that City; Fellow of the Royal Society of London; and Member of the Academies of Prussia, Stockholm, Gottingen, Turin, Padua, &c. &c.

IN FOUR VOLUMES.——WITH ELEVEN PLATES.

VOL. I.

LONDON:

PRINTED FOR G. G. AND J. ROBINSON, PATERNOSTER-ROW.

1798.

ADVERTISEMENT

BY THE

TRANSLATOR.

THE name and eſtabliſhed reputation of the Abbé Spallanzani muſt certainly be a ſufficient rcommendation of any work he gives to the public, eſpecially of one like the preſent, on which he appears to have beſtowed a more than ordinary degree of labour and attention. The variety of objects, highly intereſting to the naturaliſt and the philoſopher, on which it treats, may be ſeen in the following introduction, which contains, in part, a ſummary of the work.

ADVERTISEMENT

In the tranflation, fidelity and accuracy have been principally ftudied. The reader, it is prefumed, has before him a faithful tranfcript of the original (if the expreffion may be allowed) in his own language. Where the meaning admitted of no doubt, the tranflator thought himfelf at liberty to depart from the phrafeology of his author, to give his idea with greater perfpicuity; a licence which the different idioms of language will frequently render neceffary: but where any fhadow of ambiguity appeared (and in every work, efpecially works of fcience, fuch ambiguities of expreffion will occafionally be found) he has fcrupuloufly adhered to the literal expreffion of his text, that the reader may be enabled to form his judgment in the fame manner as from the original.

As the Abbé has continually employed

the

the terms of what is called the new nomenclature of chemiſtry; it has been thought proper, for the benefit of readers not familiar with this ſcience, to add, in a parentheſis, the more uſual names of chemical ſubſtances; as for inſtance, to ſubjoin to *muriate of alumine* the common term of *alum*; and to *muriate of ſoda* that of *ſea-ſalt*. The Abbé has likewiſe uſed the term *caloric*, on all occaſions, inſtead of heat or warmth. In this the tranſlator has not judged it adviſable to follow him, except when he has employed it in the proper chemical ſenſe of the *matter of heat*.

The plates are faithful copies of thoſe in the original, but more carefully and elegantly finiſhed. Some may, perhaps, object to the diſproportionate ſize of the human figures repreſented in plates II. III. and V. This objection the author has foreſeen, and,

at

ADVERTISEMENT.

at the end of Vol. IV. apologizes, by remarking, that " the painter conceived he might be permitted this licence, as, had he attempted to obferve the rules of proportion, thefe figures would have been fcarcely difcernible."

The work in the original is dedicated to Count Wilzeck, Imperial Plenipotentiary of the General Adminiftration of Auftrian Lombardy; but as this Dedication only contains the eulogiums of which fuch compofitions ufually confift, it has been omitted.

CONTENTS

OF THE

FIRST VOLUME.

         Page

CHAP. I.—*VISIT to Vesuvius during the Time of an Eruption* — 1

CHAP. II.—*The Grotto of Posilipo—Solfatara—The Pisciarelli* — 40

CHAP. III.—*The Grotto del Cane* — 90

CHAP. IV.—*Lakes of Agnano and Averno—Monte Nuovo—Promontory and Cavern of Miseno—Rock of Burnt Stones—Procida* — 124

CHAP. V.—*Ischia* —   — 143

CONTENTS.

	Page
CHAP. VI.—*The Valley of Metelona, near Caserta*	186
CHAP. VII.—*Journey to Mount Etna*	193
CHAP. VIII.—*Continuation of the Journey to Etna*	231
CHAP. IX.—*Return from Mount Etna to Catania*	286

INTRODUCTION.

THE zeal with which I have always been animated to contribute, as much as might be in my power, to the improvement of the Public Imperial Mufeum of Natural Hiftory in the Univerfity of Pavia, by enriching it with the new and important productions I procured in the various journeys and voyages I undertook both in Italy and other countries, incited me to travel, during the fummer and autumn vacations, into the Two Sicilies. Though this Mufeum abounded in other kinds of natural productions, it was extremely deficient

ficient in volcanic matters, which merely confifted of a few trivial fcoriæ of Vefuvius, and fome extremely common lavas of the fame mountain, that having been cut into tablets and polifhed had loft their diftinguifhing charaƈteriftics, and confequently could little contribute to the inftruƈtion of youth and the advancement of knowledge.

As I knew that no countries in Europe could furnifh a more ample and valuable colleƈtion of volcanic produƈts than the Phlegrean Fields, Mount Etna, and the Eolian, or Lipari, Ifles; I refolved to vifit them, and employed feveral months in laborious but ufeful refearches. To make a proper choice, however, of the fubftances fuitable to the defign I had in view, it was neceffary to examine on the fpot the various qualities of the bodies compofing thofe volcanized regions. This I performed with
the

the same diligence and care I have usually exerted in the examination of other natural objects. Still more to enable myself to make this selection, and correct my judgment with respect to these subjects, I had read, and then re-perused, whatever had been written by travellers and the most eminent naturalists relative to volcanos, and was sincerely grateful to them for the instruction I derived from their works. In the course of this enquiry, however, I discovered what I had often experienced before, with respect to other subjects, in which I had been preceded by other naturalists, that notwithstanding the elegant and interesting accounts they had given us of the countries which have suffered the action of fire, it was still possible to add to them by my researches, and throw new light on volcanic knowledge. This I say not to arrogate to myself any merit, and still less to

detract

detract from that of others. The powers of the human mind are so limited, that it never can entirely exhaust the subject it investigates. Other naturalists who shall hereafter diligently explore the countries through which I travelled, it is not to be doubted, may improve this part of Natural History with still new discoveries. In like manner, though others have written of the Phlegrean Fields, Etna, and the Eolian Isles, the observations I have made appear to me to merit publication.

The method in which I prosecuted my researches in these travels was the following: I have endeavoured to study volcanic countries as mountains should be studied. The lithologist who would acquire an accurate knowledge of the latter, attentively considers their structure of rock, the whole of their huge masses, the position and direction

tion of the various parts or strata which compose them, and the intertexture and relations of thofe strata. I have adopted the fame mode of enquiry in the courfe of thefe travels. Fire in conjunction with elaftic gafes has formed whole mountains and iflands; but all of them have not been produced in the fame manner, nor are they compofed of the fame fubftance. Here we find large maffes of tufa; there of fcoriæ and lavas; in another part, pumices, enamels, and glaffes; and in another a mixture of all thefe fubftances. It was therefore neceffary to examine them on the fpot, and obferve, both when they were feparate and intermingled, their relations, directions, mixtures, &c. without once lofing fight of the peculiar compofition of thefe volcanic mountains, every part and recefs of which it was requifite I fhould explore.

— In thefe enquiries I particularly directed my notice to two objects: the central summit of the iflands and mountains, and their fhores. The former is ufually the firft fenfible effect of the fubterranean conflagrations, the part which firft emerges from the waves, which often preferves the crater entire, and fometimes burning, but more frequently only its recognizable traces. The fhores of volcanic iflands and mountains bathed by the fea, were alfo peculiarly entitled to attention, nor do I know that any volcanift who has hitherto travelled has made them one of the objects of his enquiry. We know how much it conduces to an accurate knowledge of the ftructure of mountains, to crofs, or go round them in the beds of torrents which have corroded their foundations, and laid bare a part of their fides; thus revealing, if I may ufe the

the expreffion, their internal organization, which without this aid would have been fought in vain from external appearances. The fea, by inceffantly beating with its furious waves the fkirts of the iflands, has caufed fractures and ravages incomparably greater than thofe occafioned by rivers. By coafting, therefore, thefe fhores in a boat, landing where they appear to invite particular attention, and examining their open fides, and rocks half fallen down and falling, we may obferve a variety of important facts conducive to the improvement of that kind of fcience. I fhall not here enlarge on the advantages to be derived from coafting volcanic iflands; in the courfe of this work they will be proved by facts.

The refearches I made in volcanic countries, though neceffary, and highly inftructive, were not, however, sufficient to complete

plete my design. As lithologists are not satisfied with knowing the structure, stratification, and other general qualities of mountains, but endeavour likewise to discover the nature of their component parts, I resolved not to depart from the same method of enquiry. It is true that some volcanic productions are so altered by the fire, that it is difficult to ascertain the nature of the earths from which they have been produced, unless we call in aid the processes of chemistry. Such are enamels, glasses, and frequently pumices. But lavas, which, in the greater part of the places where I made my observations, are abundant beyond all belief, are seldom so changed by the fire as not to retain the evident characters of their primitive rocks.

I began, then, by considering the external appearance and qualities of the places I ex-

I examined, as far, at leaft, as circumftances would permit.

Whoever has undertaken to travel among mountains, in order to make refearches relative to the foffil kingdom, is not ignorant to what changes the furfaces of ftony fubftances, even the moft folid and hard, are fubject, from the action of the elements during a long feries of years and ages. Hence, if he would form an accurate judgment of the ftones he examines, he will not fix his attention on thofe found on the furface of the earth, but rather on thofe buried at fome depth, and will frequently forcibly break and detach them from the internal maffes of which they are a continuation. Still greater changes take place in fome parts of the mountains which throw out fire, from the action of fulphureous-acid vapours, befides that of the atmofphere and of time; and very frequently the volcanic product, which on the surface seems to be of one kind, and at some depth of another, is in fact the same, but more or less changed in the first instance by the action of the atmosphere, or that of sulphureous vapours.

— — To render my researches more accurate and certain, it was necessary that I should not content myself with a single inspection of the volcanic substances, on the spot where I gathered them. I therefore, when I returned to Pavia, re-examined them with the greatest care, in the retirement of my study; not only with the naked eye, but with the aid of the lens, before I began to characterize and describe them lithologically. The reader will find some of the descriptions rather diffuse; and, perhaps, I may be charged with having been too minute.

But it appeared to me that I could not be more concife; as a detailed defcription of fuch products can alone enable us to difcover to what kind of rocks they appertain, and what is the particular characteriftic of the volcanic countries in which they are found. Thofe who, when treating of volcanos, have been fparing of fuch defcriptions, have left us imperfect works, though in other refpects they may be very valuable. All who are verfed in thefe fubjects, are acquainted with the account of the famous eruption of Etna in 1669, and the memoirs relative to different remarkable conflagrations of Vefuvius by Serao, Della Torre, Sir William Hamilton, and Bottis. With refpect to what regards the currents of lava which thofe two volcanos at thofe times poured forth, the fymptoms and phenomena that accompanied them, and the other circumftances deferving notice which

preceded

preceded and followed them, their histories certainly merit great commendation. They will be highly valuable in the estimation of every lover of volcanic science; and I have frequently, in the course of this work, derived such assistance from them as demands my grateful acknowledgment. But from these relations, what idea can we in general form of the nature of the products ejected and the currents they have formed? When do they describe with sufficient accuracy a single substance? After having read these relations of the violent eruptions which have burst from the sides of Vesuvius and Etna, we remain profoundly ignorant to what primitive rocks they appertain. I mean not by these remarks to injure the reputation these writers have justly acquired. Their deficiency in lithological studies, not cultivated at that time as in the present, is a sufficient excuse; I intend only to shew the necessity

necessity there is for circumstantial descriptions, which, in fact, form the basis of all solid science.

It is necessary that I should here mention, with respect to the descriptions I have given of the different products of the various volcanic places I visited, that, though I have treated diffusely, and in detail, of those of the Phlegrean Fields, situated to the west of Naples, and of others of the Eolian or Lipari Isles; I have only spoken incidentally of the productions of Vesuvius and Etna, though both these volcanos have furnished me with a great number of specimens for the Museum at Pavia; not only because that to have examined these two mountains minutely, would have required years instead of a few months; but because a description of these has already been executed with great ability by the Chevalier Gioeni, in his

Lithologia

—*Lithologia Vesuviana*, and by M. Dolomieu, in his " Descriptive Catalogue of the Pro- " ducts of Etna."

The opportunity afforded me by having these volcanic substances continually under my inspection at Pavia, induced me to make new experiments on them. It is certain, that the greater part of them contain iron. Yet the proof of this by experiment was not superfluous, as the greater or less quantity of the martial principle might thus be discovered. I therefore used, according to circumstances, the magnetic needle, or magnetized knife. I applied the former to the products reduced to powder, and the latter to those in fragments; taking care that they should always be, as far as I was able to effect it, of the same configuration and volume. I then observed the different distances at which they attracted the magnetic needle,

needle, without noticing the pieces which exerted no fuch power, though I do not mean by that to deny that they contained iron*.

I was attentive at the fame time to an enquiry of much greater importance. Vefuvius, Etna, the Eolian Ifles, and Ifchia, are large mountains formed of rocks which have undergone liquefaction, and fometimes a true vitrification; fuch has been the violence of the fubterranean conflagrations. What fire can we produce equivalent to thefe effects? I have difcovered that the fire of the glafs-furnace will completely refufe the vitrifications, enamels, pumices, fcoriæ, and lavas of thefe and other volcanic countries. The fame will, in like manner, vitrify rocks con-

* As the iron is fometimes in the ftate of oxyde (calx), I employed the ufual methods to revive it in the productions I examined.

generous

generous to thofe from which thefe mountains have originated by the means of fubterranean conflagrations. A lefs intenfe fire, on the contrary, produces no fuch effect on any of thefe fubftances.

As I wifhed to attain to the moft rigorous accuracy in this experiment, I was not fatisfied with difcovering that the fire of the glafs-furnace was capable of effecting thefe fufions; I determined, if poffible, to afcertain the precife degree of heat neceffary to produce them, for which purpofe nothing could be better adapted than the pyrometer of Wedgwood. This inftrument, it is well known, is compofed of two parts; the thermometric pieces and the gage. The former are fmall cylinders of very fine clay. The latter, which is fix inches long, is formed by two pieces of the fame earth, the internal fides of which are ftraight and fmooth, smooth; but so disposed as to be more distant from each other at one extremity than the other, thus forming a converging space divided into 240 parts. The greater aperture of this gage is the beginning of the scale, and denotes the heat which produces a beginning of redness in iron. If, therefore, one of the clay cylinders shall have been exposed to a greater heat, it will be contracted, and sink lower between the converging sides; and, the sides being graduated, the degree at which it stops will be the measure of its contraction, and consequently of the degree of heat it has undergone; the cylinders, as the inventor has observed, representing the mercury, and the converging sides the scale of the thermometer.

To ascertain, therefore, the degree of heat in the glass furnace necessary for the fusion of these volcanic productions, and the rocks whence they derive their origin, I made ufe of this pyrometer in the following manner. I placed in the furnace, near the fubftances I intended to fufe, one or more of the clay cylinders abovementioned, in a cafe of the fame clay, and let them remain there the whole time neceffary for the fufion of thofe fubftances. I then meafured their contraction by the gage; and found that the heat of the glafs furnace was $87\frac{1}{8}$ degrees of this pyrometer; a heat, according to the obfervation of the inventor, but $2\frac{1}{2}$ degrees lefs than that of welding iron, which latter heat correfponds to $12777°$ of Fahrenheit's thermometer[*]. In fact, filings of iron (in which the furface of the metal is greatly enlarged) being continued four-and-twenty hours in the glafs furnaces of Pavia, of which I always made ufe in thefe experiments, conglutinated into a folid though friable

[*] Journal de Rozier, tom. xxx.

body,

body, and shewed an evident beginning fusion. Whence I conclude that a greater heat is usually kept up in these furnaces than is necessary for the fusion of glass.

Though the blowing pipe did not in general greatly conduce to the success of my experiments, I sometimes found it useful. In some cases I likewise had recourse to the assistance of fire excited by oxygenous gas (dephlogisticated air).

There is scarcely any natural product, volcanic or not volcanic, of which I have treated in this work, that I did not try in the fire, in one or other of the manners I have described, and frequently more than once. These experiments in the dry way I often accompanied with others in the humid, with respect to the productions of volcanic fire.

The manner in which I proceeded was as follows:

When the external appearance of thefe products perfectly agreed with that of earths not volcanic before known, and analyfed by able chemifts; I thought I might determine the genus of the volcanic production without analyzing it in the humid way; and when I made experiments on a few pieces, I found I was not deceived. But when the external appearance appeared to me new, and not to agree with that of the earths already known, I then had recourfe to an examination by the humid method, by which I elucidated the genus, and frequently the fpecies, of thefe fubftances. Before, therefore, I proceeded to defcribe any pieces I had collected, I was certain, or thought myfelf fo, that I had obtained a fufficient knowledge of them. And when I could

I could not arrive at this knowldge, but remained uncertain to what genus they appertained, I have never failed to expreſs myſelf doubtfully. In theſe reſearches, equally laborious, delicate, and neceſſary, I have employed much of my time, not without conſiderable expence. In my volcanic travels I have been obliged to take upon myſelf the parts both of naturaliſt and chemiſt. The natural hiſtory of foſſils is ſo cloſely connected with modern chemiſtry, and the rapid and prodigious progreſs of the one ſo exactly keeps pace with that of the other, that we cannot ſeparate them without great injury to both. But as the chemiſt in his laboratory can reaſon but imperfectly concerning the mountains, the component earth of which he analyzes; ſo the obſervations of the lithological traveller muſt always be defective when not conjoined (at leaſt when it may be neceſſary) with chemical inveſtigations.

tions. What is true of fossils not volcanic, must likewise be so, in a certain degree, and with necessary allowances, of volcanic fossils. Here, in fine, neither observation alone, nor experience alone, are sufficient; but both must join to conduct the investigator of nature, or he cannot be successful in his researches.

Where my experimental enquiries have been short, I have incorporated them with my narrative; as they are relative to the productions I met with in the different places I visited. But more than once I have found it convenient to act otherwise; and the subjects treated, appear to me to justify the method I have adopted.

What is the activity, in general, of volcanic fires, has been a question long agitated, and which is certainly of difficult solution.

In

In this dispute, writers have gone into opposite extremes; some asserting that these fires are extremely active, and others that they are very feeble, while all endeavour to support their opinions by facts. Having treated on volcanos so much at length in this work, I could not avoid considering this question. I have weighed the arguments on both sides without prejudice; I have made various experiments; and declared in favour of the opinion which appeared to me to have the strongest support from reason and from facts.

The nature of elastic gases by which the liquefied matters of volcanos are penetrated and agitated, was another subject well deserving attentive consideration. The vacuities, inflations, and tumors, which such matters frequently retain in a state of congelation, can only be ascribed to the elasticity of these gases while they were in a state of liquidity.

quidity. Our common fire will reproduce in them thefe gafes equally with the volcanic. In fact, many lavas, pumices, glaffes, enamels, and fcoriæ, though by pulverization they may be deprived of thefe vacuities, which are more or lefs large, and ufually orbicular, recover them by refufion in the furnace; and in many of thefe bodies the gafeous bubbles are fo abundant, that by their great inflation, while in actual fufion, they force them to flow over the edges of the crucible. Thefe obfervations led the way to enquiries relative to the qualities of thefe gafes, by liquefying in chemical furnaces volcanic fubftances reduced to powder, and placed in matraffes fitted to a chemical mercurial apparatus. By a great number of experiments of this kind I difcovered the true nature of thefe gafeous fubftances, of which our knowledge was before very vague and uncertain.

This

This discovery naturally led to the enquiry what part the elastic gases take in the eruptions of volcanos; and this enquiry to a discussion of the causes of those eruptions.

The chemical processes I employed to ascertain the characters of the gases of volcanic productions likewise discovered to me a new fact, which was, that several of these productions contain muriatic acid. This discovery again produced new enquiries[*].

Lastly, I must not omit the researches relative to the origin of prismatic or basaltiform lavas. It is an opinion almost universal, that lavas take this regular figure in the sea,

[*] In these chemical experiments I was greatly assisted by the Signors Nocetti, father and son; the former operator in the public school of chemistry in Pavia, and the latter repeater in the same. They are both well versed in chemical science, and are entitled to my grateful acknowledgments.

by the sudden condensation and congelation they suffered when they flowed into it in a fluid state. I could not have met with examples of this kind more proper to enable me to form a judgment on the subject than those which presented themselves to my view while coasting the shores of Italy, a great part of Etna, and the whole of the Lipari islands.

These different discussions relative to the efficacy of subterraneous conflagrations, the gases of volcanic productions, the causes of the eruptions of volcanos, and the muriatic acid contained in various of their products; with the enquiries concerning the origin of basaltiform lavas—to treat them at length, as they required, would have too much broken the thread of the narrative of my travels. I have therefore placed them in such a manner as not to interfere with

with my accounts of the Phlegrean Fields, Etna, and the Eolian Isles.

In the volcanized countries in which I travelled, there are four craters still burning, Vesuvius, Etna, Stromboli, and Vulcano. To all these four, from an ardent desire of obtaining knowledge, I wished to make a near approach. By Vesuvius this wish was not gratified; but Etna was more condescending, though incomparably more formidable; and a similar good fortune attended me at Stromboli and Vulcano. The clear and distinct view I had of these three craters was equally pleasing and instructive. The crater of Etna I delineated myself; the views of Vulcano and Stromboli are the work of a draughtsman I took with me for that purpose, and who likewise furnished me with drawings of some other volcanic mountains described in this work. I shall only add, that

that all these designs have been retouched and greatly improved by Sig. Francesco Lanfranchi, an eminent painter in the University of Pavia.

The origin of the Lipari islands, which are the productions of fire, was certainly the principal motive of my visiting them; yet in many other respects they are certainly very interesting. The character, manners, and customs of the inhabitants; their population, agriculture, and commerce, are objects well deserving enquiry; and have the greater claim to the attention of an Italian, from their being so little known in Italy.

I have also made some observations on the animals in those islands, as, for instance, on a kind of birds, which, with us, are birds of passage, but there (in part at least) stationary:

ary: I mean swallows. Some years ago I made observations on the natural qualities of several species of swallows (the *Hirundo rustica, urbica, riparia, apus, melba, Linn.*) and to these I now add those I made in the Lipari islands.

The environs of Messina, where, after I had finished my volcanic travels, I remained more than a month, afforded me much instruction from the variety of natural objects they presented. Though four years and a half had elapsed since that unfortunate city had been laid in ruins by earthquakes, the melancholy scene was still fresh in every one's memory. A great part of the public and private edifices were still in the same ruinous condition to which they were reduced by that calamitous event. Numbers of the inhabitants still continued to lodge in the half destroyed houses, and others in huts

and

and sheds; while they all appeared oppressed and overwhelmed with fears from which they had not yet recovered. The impressions made on me by what I saw of the effects of this calamity were such that I could not refrain from giving a brief account of the melancholy situation in which I found Messina, and of the destruction occasioned by the dreadful earthquake in 1783.

Scylla and Charybdis, the former distant twelve miles from Messina, and the latter about a hundred paces, within the famous Strait, were two objects to which I first turned my attention. That part of the sea being then calm, at least as calm as the Strait of Messina can be; I was enabled to take a near view of them both, and even to pass over Charybdis in a boat. I also made enquiries of the Messinese sailors, who are employed the greater part of the year in

that

that Strait, and confequently have an opportunity of forming a juft and precife idea of thefe two celebrated places; and from what they told me, and the obfervations I made myfelf, I am convinced that Charybdis is not a real whirlpool, as has been hitherto believed.

In the Strait of Meffina I found other inftructive natural curiofities furnifhed by the fifheries for the fword-fifh *(Xiphias gladius Lin.)*, the ravenous fhark *(Squalus carcharias)*, and for coral *(Ifis nobilis)*.

Being at Meffina at the time of the annual paffage of the fword-fifh through the Strait, I was prefent at the fifhery, which appeared to merit fome defcription from the fingular form of the veffels employed in it; the method of ftriking and taking the fifh; and the qualities and periodical migrations

grations of the animal. I have, likewise, made some observations on some fish of the genus of the *squalus*, particularly the shark; sometimes so dangerous to fishermen in that sea.

Coral, for which the Messinese mariners fish the whole year, by tearing it with nets suitable to the purpose from the rocks at the bottom of their Strait, has been long an ambiguous production, and made to pass through all the three kingdoms of nature; some considering it as a fossil, others as a vegetable; until, at length, it has been proved to appertain to the class of animals, though it has the appearance of a plant; and is, therefore, now properly classed among the zoophyta. The excellent observations of Peyssonel and Vitalianio Donati are well known; nor ought Marsigli to be denied the praise he merits, though

though a zealous maintainer that coral is a plant. Notwithstanding, however, these great discoveries, much was wanting to a complete history of this noble zoophyte, to which, I flatter myself, I have in some small degree contributed by the observations I made on it, at the time of the fishery, at which I was present.

On this occasion, while the fishermen were throwing the net for the coral, I employed myself in researches for marine animalcula. I carefully examined every piece of a stalk, leaf, or other fragment of a marine plant, or any thing else which hung to the net, having learned from experience that these substances sometimes contain wonders, in the class of animated beings; for, as Pliny has wisely remarked: Nature is greatest in her least productions. When the fishermen, therefore, turned up their nets to free them from the weeds which were mixed with the coral, I put thefe weeds into glafs veffels, filled with fea-water, to obferve the animals adhering to them, and felect thofe which appeared to prefent any remarkable novelty. Several of thefe were not wanting; of the genera of the *Afcidiæ* and the *Efcharæ*. I likewife difcovered fome fmall polypi, in which I could diftinctly fee the circulation of the fluids; which has not, to my knowledge, been before obferved in thefe minute animals. The defcription I have given of them is accompanied with the neceffary figures.

The furface, likewife, of the Strait of Meffina was equally favourable to my refearches with the bottom. In other parts of the Mediterranean, the Adriatic, the Archipelago, and the Strait of Conftantinople,

nople, I had examined several species of those mollusca which are commonly called medusæ. I had admired the simplicity of their organization, and especially that property by which certain species of them, of the weight of twenty pounds or more, dissolve almost entirely into a liquor; nothing remaining of them but some thin and dry pellicles, which are only a few grains in weight. I had never however met with any of that phosphorescent kind which Lœflingius tells us he saw in the ocean between Spain and America. The mention he has thus made of them, without adding any further observations, can only serve to excite the curiosity of the reader; nor do I know that any other author has described this rare animal. In the Strait of Messina I had the pleasure to find abundance of these phosphorescent mollusca, and the stay I made in that city afforded me an opportunity to examine their organization,

ganization, their motion, and the beautiful light they emit in the dark.

I concluded my refearches relative to the natural objects in the vicinity of Meffina, by examining the fhore, hills, and mountains, which on the fide oppofite the fea look toward that city. I could difcover no fign of volcanization; but I obferved, firft, immenfe maffes of teftaceous and other animals petrified, the fpecies of which were perfectly diftinguifhable. Secondly, granite, which probably is a continuation of that of Melazzo, diftant from Meffina thirty miles to the north; and with refpect to which I endeavoured to afcertain whether it formed ftrata, as fome fuppofe, or only great maffes, as is the opinion of others; as alfo whether it contained within it petrified marine bodies, as has been conjectured. Thirdly, fandftone, which, it appears to me probable,
forms,

forms, in a great meafure, the bottom of the Strait of Meffina, extending to the point Peloro, and being reproduced by a petrifying principle. We fhall fee that by means of this principle, human fkeletons, and other extraneous bodies, are fometimes found included in it; and that, in confequence of the fame, at the part near Peloro, where the Strait is narroweft, it is probable that Sicily, lofing the name of an ifland, will one day be again joined to Italy.

Having made the circuit of the Phlegrean Fields, the Eolian Ifles and Etna, the principal objects of my travels, I returned to Pavia, going by fea from Naples, without the leaft thought of making any new obfervations. But the lake of Orbitello, celebrated for the immenfe quantities of large eels (*Muræna Anguilla Linn.*) it produces, became a new incentive to my curiofity;

and

and a dead calm detaining the veffel in which I had taken my paffage feveral days at Porto Ercole, a few miles diftant from Orbitello; as I could eafily obtain as many eels as I chofe, I examined them with great attention to difcover, if poffible, the manner in which they propagate their fpecies, fince, notwithftanding the numerous experiments that have been made both by ancient and modern naturalifts to elucidate this queftion, it is not yet known with certainty whether they are viviparous or oviparous. To the experiments I now made, when I returned into Lombardy, I added many others in the following years, made in every feafon.

With this view, exprefsly, I repaired to the lakes of Comacchio, which, with that abovementioned, abound more with this fifh than any in Europe. I here affiduoufly ftudied the various qualities of the animal, in order

order to illustrate its history, which is in many respects deficient and obscure.

The last place at which I landed before my arrival at Genoa, was the island of Elba, where I was obliged to remain five days in consequence of another calm. I profited by this delay to visit the ancient and celebrated iron mines, where I procured for the Imperial Museum at Pavia some noble specimens of that metal crystallized, and augmented the copious collection I carried with me with some sulphures of iron (pyrites).

I returned to the University about the end of the year 1788, having employed six months in my travels in the two Sicilies; with which, though they were at my own expence, like the greater part of my other travels, I am well satisfied, since I have been able to contribute something to that noble public inftitution the Mufeum at Pavia; but my fatisfaction will be ftill greater, if the work I now prefent to the public be approved by its readers.

Thus I employed the fummer and autumnal vacations of that year. Some time before, but efpecially in the vacations of 1789 and 1790, I made refearches among the mountains of Modena and Reggio, with refpect to objects which, as they have a relation to volcanos, may have a place in this work.

The fires of Barigazzo, which burn on the Apennines of Modena, have been long known. Thefe confift of groups of feeble flames collected in a narrow fpace, which rife above the earth, are almoft always vifible, and, if by chance they become extinct, may be rekindled by bringing a fmall flame to the fpot where they were. The accounts

accounts of them, however, are so few, and so defective, that, at most, they can only serve to compare the present state of these flames with what it once was. The light afforded by modern physics enables us to affirm, without farther examination, that the cause of this feeble fire must be hydrogenous gas (or inflammable gas). I made a journey to Barigazzo purposely to ascertain this, and found it to be the fact. In that vicinity there are six other similar fires, at present only known to the Alpine peasants, all originating from the same principle.

But in the present accurate state of our knowledge relative to aëriform gases, it is too little to say and prove that the cause of these various flames is hydrogenous gas. The following are the principal enquiries which I think it necessary for me, as a naturalist, to make with respect to these fires,

and

and such objects as may have a relation to them.

First, to examine the structure and composition of those mountains; and here I shall incidentally have occasion to speak of *Cimone*, not far distant from Barigazzo, and the highest mountain of our Apennines.

Secondly, carefully to remark the qualities of each of these fires, and the phenomena accompanying them.

Thirdly, to compare these fires nourished by natural hydrogenous gas, with those produced by hydrogenous gas procured by art.

Fourthly, to make a rigorous analysis of the hydrogenous gas of the fires of Barigazzo and the other neighbouring places,

by

by means of the chemical mercurial apparatus; and to carry to thofe Alpine heights veffels to contain the different aëriform fluids, and inftruments neceffary for thefe analyfes.

Fifthly, to make the fame analyfis of the earths from which thefe fires arife. And here I muft obferve by the way, that having made at Barigazzo an excavation of fome depth and fize, in order to obtain the earth pure; the fires multiplied fo much, and became fo powerful, that, after I had left the place, the hollow was employed as a furnace for lime, and lime-ftone as perfectly burnt in it as in furnaces prepared for the purpofe.

Sixthly, to examine what may be the matters generative of this inexhauftible fupply of hydrogenous gas; which has been fo long continually developed; it being
certain,

certain, from authentic documents, that these fires have burned for a century and a half.

In the hills of Modena and Reggio we find certain places which the people of the country call *Salse*, and which are a kind of volcanos in miniature; having the form externally of the truncated cone, and, internally, of the inverted funnel. They sometimes throw up into the air earthy matters; which at other times overflow, and, pouring down their sides, form small currents. After the manner of burning mountains, they frequently open with several mouths; and like them rage, thunder, and cause slight earthquakes around them. But in the true volcanos the primary agent is fire; in these *Salse* the generative principle is entirely different.

Some of them have hitherto remained wholly unknown to naturalists: of others authors have written, but have described the phenomena with little accuracy and frequent exaggeration; not to mention that, at the time when they wrote, the nature of the agent from which these phenomena derive their origin was not discovered.

These *Salse* have claimed my attention equally with the fires abovementioned; and I have applied myself to study them with equal assiduity, and with the same chemical analysis; and as they both, after the manner of volcanos, undergo changes which appear sometimes to have relation to those of the atmosphere, I have judged it necessary frequently to visit them, and in different seasons, to observe the various phenomena, and with more certainty discover the secret causes to which they owe their origin.

The Travels I now present to the public, and of which I have here given the summary, will be speedily followed by another work containing an account of my voyages to Constantinople, in the Mediterranean, and in the Adriatic.

ERRATA.

VOL. I.

Page	Line	
46	20	*after* paonazzo, *read*, or purple colour.
—	22	*for* vitrifactions *read* vitrifications.
58	10	*for* oxyde of yellow iron *read* yellow oxyde of iron.
124	15	*for* smalt *read* enamel.
163	11	*dele* other.
174	23	*for* native iron *read* specular iron.

VOL. II.

65	13	*for* the lava *read* as the lava.
209	16	*for* likewise suffered *read* likewise had suffered.

VOL. III.

306	2	*dele* of.

TRAVELS

IN THE

TWO SICILIES, &c.

CHAP. I.

A VISIT TO VESUVIUS DURING THE TIME OF AN ERUPTION.

Little notice taken by the Neapolitans of the smaller eruptions of this volcano—Phenomena observed by the author on his arrival at Naples—His approach near to the crater prevented by showers of ignited stones, and acid-sulphureous fumes—Extraordinary phenomenon relative to these showers—Explication of that phenomenon—Remarks on the congelation of a torrent of lava—Observations on a stream of lava flowing within a cavern—Projected experiment for measuring the quantity of heat in the flowing lava—Other observations on the lava issuing from a subterraneous cavity—Remarkable cataract formed by it in its passage—Length, breadth, and termination of this torrent—Phenomena of this eruption of Vesuvius compared with those of preceding ones—Erroneous opinion of some naturalists, that the lava is not fluid, but of the consistence of paste—Composition of this lava—Observations on a lava of Vesuvius which flowed in 1785—Proofs that the shoerls and feltspars found in the lava existed previously in the primordial rocks.

WHEN I arrived at Naples, on the 24th of July 1788, though Vesuvius was not in a state of inactivity, its conflagration was not sufficient to excite the curiosity of the Neapolitans; who, from having it continually before their eyes, are seldom inclined to visit it, but during its great and destructive eruptions.

tions. At that time, during the day, it without intermiffion fent forth fmoke, which rifing formed a white cloud round the fummit, and, being driven by the northeaft wind, extended in a long ftream to the ifland of Capri. By night, repeated eruptions of fire were vifible, though no fubterraneous explofions were to be heard at Naples; and a tract of ground to the fouth of the crater affumed a dufky red colour, which, by the experienced in volcanic phenomena, was faid to be preparatory to the flowing of the lava. I fhould immediately have repaired to the place, had not my friends at Naples affured me, from the practical knowledge they had of their burning mountain, that that eruption, which at my arrival was but inconfiderable, would after fome time become much more extenfive. It was in fact my wifh to fee Vefuvius, if not raging with its moft tremendous fury, at leaft in a more than ordinary commotion.

I, in confequence, returned from Sicily to Naples in the beginning of November, when

a ftream

a ſtream of lava, iſſuing from an aperture in the ſide of the mountain, covered a conſiderable extent of ground, and began to be viſible before day-light, from beyond Capri, under the appearance of a ſtreak of a reddiſh colour. On the 4th of the ſame month, I began my journey to the volcano, and paſſed the night at the Hermitage del Salvatore, two miles from the ſummit of the mountain. Before I retired to reſt, I paſſed ſeveral hours in making obſervations with the greateſt attention; nor could the opportunity have been more favourable, as there was no moon, and the ſky was perfectly free from clouds.

I had therefore a clear view of the eruptions of the mountain, which had the appearance of a red flame, that enlarged as it roſe, continued a few ſeconds, and then diſappeared. The ejections ſucceeded each other at unequal intervals of time; but no intermiſſion continued longer than five minutes.

I roſe

I rose four hours before day, and continued my journey towards the burning crater, from which, as I have before said, flames arose at intervals, which on a nearer approach appeared larger and more vivid; and every ejection was followed by a detonation, more or less loud, according to the quantity of burning matter ejected: a circumstance I did not notice before, on account of the distance, but which became more perceptible to the ear in proportion as I approached the mouth of the volcano; and I observed, when I had arrived within half a mile of it, in a direct line, that the ejections preceded their accompanying explosions only by an instant, which is agreeable to the laws of the propagation of light and sound. At this distance not only flames were visible to the eye, but a shower of ignited stones, which, in the stronger ejections, were thrown to a prodigious height, and thence fell on the declivities of the mountain, emitting a great quantity of vivid sparks, and bounding and rolling till they came within a short distance of the place where I stood.

These stones, when I afterwards examined them, I found to be only particles of the lava, which had become solid in the air, and taken a globose form. These showers of lava appeared an invincible obstacle to my nearer approach to the volcanic furnace. I did not, however, lose all hope, being encouraged by the following observation. The showers of heated stones, I remarked, did not fall vertically, but all inclined a little to the west. I therefore removed to the east side of Vesuvius, where I could approach nearer to the burning mouth: but a wind suddenly springing up from the west, compelled me to remove, with no little regret, to a greater distance, as the smoke from the mouth of the crater, which before rose in a perpendicular column, was now drifted by the wind to the side on which I stood; so that I soon found myself enveloped in a cloud of smoke abounding with sulphureous vapours, and was obliged hastily to retire down the side of the mountain. Yet though I was thus disappointed of the pleasure of approaching nearer to the edge of the crater,

and

and obferving the eruptions more nearly and accurately, many inftructive objects were not wanting. But before I proceed to any remarks on thefe, I muft notice a curious and unexpected circumftance.

I have already fpoken of the detonations which accompanied the fhowers of lava. It is now neceffary to add, that thefe did not conftantly accompany every eruption. When I had taken my ftation in the lower part of the mountain, I found the detonations more fenfible, and refembling the noife produced by a large mine when it explodes; but fuddenly, to my great furprife, they ceafed, though the ejections of fiery matter continued both frequent and copious. I counted eighteen eruptions which were not accompanied by the fmalleft noife. The nineteenth, though not larger than the former, was followed by its detonation, as were eleven more, though others which fucceeded were filent. This irregularity I obferved fo repeatedly, that the detonations appeared to me rather accidental than neceffarily cessarily connected with the explosions. In this opinion I am supported by the authority of my ingenious friend, the Abbé Fortis, who afterwards told me, at Naples, that he had frequently observed the same inconstancy in the eruptions of Vesuvius.

This peculiar phenomenon, which has not, to my knowledge, been remarked by any one of the numerous authors who have written on Vesuvius, does not appear, at first view, to be easily explicable from the physical cause of the explosions. As it must be allowed that the fire alone is not sufficient to produce it, we must have recourse to an elastic fluid, which disengages itself from the lava, impelling at the same time a part of it into the air; which effect can scarcely happen without a detonation. But on more mature reflection it appeared to me most probable that this takes place only within certain limits. When the elastic fluid bursts suddenly against the lava, it is to be expected that it will produce a considerable report; but when it acts slowly it will occasion little or none, hone, though the ejection may be very ſtrong. Thus, if the atmoſpheric air be confined between two pellets of tow in a tube, and one of them be forced ſuddenly towards the other, the latter will be projected to ſome diſtance, with a confiderable found, but none, or very little, will be heard if the pellet be gradually preſſed towards the other. In like manner, the air contained in an air-gun produces ſcarcely any report on its difcharge, on account of the interpoſition of the valve delaying its action on the ball.

In what I have ſaid, however, I do not mean to aſſert that theſe volcanic eruptions were entirely unaccompanied with any exploſive found. It is highly probable they were not; but that I could not hear the feebler detonations on account of the diſtance.

It has been already ſaid, that the liquid lava had opened itſelf a way, not immediately from the ſummit of the crater, but from one ſide of the mountain. The following

lowing are the obfervations made on this fubject. Towards the fouth-eaft, at the diftance of about half a mile from the crater, on a declivity, there arofe fixty or more fmall columns of fmoke, one of which was about nine feet in diameter, and came from a not very deep cavern. The ground from which thefe ftreams of fmoke iffued was tinged with yellow, from the muriate of ammoniac, and fo hot, that, even at fome diftance, I could bear my feet on it only for a few feconds. It is fufficiently manifeft that the fmoke and the heat proceeded from the fame caufe; that is to fay, from the fubterraneous conflagration which communicated with that part, and caufed the fmoke to burft forth through the fiffures in the ground.

At the diftance of a few paces from this fpot, the aperture was vifible through which, fix months before, the lava difgorged itfelf, as I was affured by my guide; but it no longer flowed at the time of my arrival, its current having acquired the hardnefs of ftone.

stone. About fifty paces lower, however, in the same direction, that is towards the south, the lava was still running within a kind of pit, but without rising above its borders; and at a place still lower, about two miles from the principal crater of Vesuvius, the lava issued from the subterranean cavern, forming in the open air a long current. But before I proceed to describe the latter, it will be proper to notice the highly curious phenomena observable in the lava moving within the above-mentioned cavity or pit. This pit was of a shape approaching to an oval, about twenty-three feet in circuit. The sides, or banks, were nearly perpendicular, about four feet and a half in height; and it was excavated in the hardened lava of the last eruption. The burning lava moved within this cavern, of which it covered the whole bottom, in the direction of from north to south. From it arose a cloud of smoke, which, reflecting the light from the red hot lava, produced in the air a red brightness, that during the night might be seen at a considerable distance. But as this smoke was strongly impregnated with acid-sulphureous vapours, I found it a great obstacle to my making any observations on the liquid lava, when, from the calmness of the air, it ascended perpendicularly. But, from time to time, a slight breeze arose which carried the stream towards one side; and I then removed to the opposite, where I was no longer incommoded in my experiments by the vapour. During these favourable intervals, I could stoop down towards the pit, in which I observed the appearances which I here faithfully relate.

As the distance between the lower extremities of my body and the lava was only five feet, the heat it sent forth was very vehement, but not absolutely intolerable, though it forced me to remove from it a little, from time to time.

I observed, then, that the lava flowed, as I have before said, along this cavity, from the north to the south, and then disappeared under the excavated hardened lava. Its
surface

surface exhibited the redness of burning coal, but without the smallest appearance of flame. I know nothing to which it can be more properly compared than melted brass in a furnace. This superficies was in some places covered with a white froth; and from time to time bubbles arose in it, which burst a moment after with a sensible noise. Sometimes, likewise, the lava rose in small jets or spouts, which, in an instant after, subsided, and the surface again became smooth and even.

The nearness of my approach to this melted matter, which I observed, first, during the darkness of the night, and afterwards by the light of day, removed every shade of doubt or uncertainty respecting the remarks I made. It likewise furnished me with an opportunity to make some experiments which I otherwise could not have made. I was desirous to let fall some heavy body into the flowing lava; but my situation would only permit me to use, for this purpose, pieces of lava which lay round the cavern, as I could find no substance of any
other

other kind. When I threw thefe pieces into the lava, they occafioned that dull kind of found which would have been produced by ftriking foft earth or thick mud; and at the fame time formed in the lava an incavation, in which they were buried about one third part of their bulk, and in this fituation were carried away by the current. The fame happened when I, at other times, ufed larger pieces, and threw them forcibly into the lava; the only difference was that then they funk in deeper.

From this experiment I afcertained the velocity of the lava, as it is certain that muft have been the fame with that of the ftone carried by it. In about half a minute, the pieces of folid lava were carried ten feet and a half. The motion of the current was therefore very flow; which was not furprifing, as the declivity was very little. We fhall fee prefently, that the pieces of lava with which I made my experiment, were probably of the fame kind with the lava which was flowing; on which account I, at firſt, expected that they would have ſunk entirely within it, ſince it is well known that all bodies which paſs from a fluid to a ſolid ſtate become more compact; but a moment's reflection convinced me that the fact could happen no otherwiſe than it did. The pieces of lava which I threw into the current were full of pores and cavities, which in the liquid lava could not have place, or at leaſt could not be ſo numerous: theſe pieces, therefore, muſt be lighter than the liquid lava. Another reaſon, which I conſider as ſtill more deciſive, is derived from the tenacious liquidity of the flowing lava, which muſt prevent the entire immerſion of the ſolid lava, though the latter ſhould be ſpecifically heavier. Thus I have obſerved, that a ſolid globe of glaſs, though thrown with ſome force into a liquid maſs of the ſame matter, will not remain entirely ſubmerged, but float with a part above the ſurface.

I would willingly have made another experiment, which I ſhould have conſidered as of much greater importance; but I had not

not with me the inftruments neceffary to undertake it; becaufe I had not the leaft expectation that I fhould have been able to approach fo near to the flowing lava as would have given me an opportunity to have ufed them.

The experiment I mean was to have afcertained the degree of abfolute heat of the flowing lava, and might have been very conveniently made at this place. As therefore circumftances did not permit me to make a fecond vifit to Vefuvius, and as thefe cavities which receive into them the flowing lava are frequently met with in volcanic eruptions, it may not be improper here to detail the nature and mode of the experiments I would have made, had I been furnifhed with the neceffary means, in hope that fome fimilar opportunity may induce fome one of the few naturalifts of Naples who are defirous to enlarge the knowledge we have of their volcano, to carry them into effect.

Firft,

First, therefore, I would have let fall on the lava within that cavity two kinds of substances, inflammable and fusible, contriving some means to keep them fixed in the same place; punctually noticing the time required for the inflaming of the former and the fusion of the latter. I would then have exposed the same substances to our common fires, until the same effects had been produced, observing the difference of time between the production of the effect by the volcanic fire and the common. I should thus have obtained a term of comparison of great utility in the enquiry proposed. But a method more precise and certain would be to make use of the pyrometer of Mr. Wedgwood *; which should be used in the following manner. To ascertain the absolute heat of the superficies of the lava, one or more of the cylinders of clay should be let down upon it, enclosed in the box of the same earth adapted to them, fastened to an iron chain that it may not be carried away by the current, and the expe-

* See the Introduction.

riment prevented. This being taken up, after having been fuffered to remain there fome hours, the fhortening of the cylinders would fhew the quantity of abfolute heat they had fuffered, and, confequently, that of the lava on which they had refted.

But with this experiment alone I fhould not have been entirely fatisfied. By the affiftance of this fame pyrometer, I would have endeavoured to difcover the internal abfolute heat of the lava, by immerging within it fome of the cylinders I have before mentioned, enclofed in a thick hollow globe of iron, faftened to a chain of the fame metal. The infufibility of iron in our common furnaces inclines me to believe that it would refift the heat of the liquid lava; but fhould it not, its melting would fupply the place of a pyrometer, and fufficiently prove the violence of the heat.

I am aware that thefe experiments would not afcertain, with precifion, the heat of other torrents of lava, which muft necessarily

rily depend on the greater or less depth of the ignited matter, its distance from the principal seat of the conflagration, and the different qualities of the lava. But they must have been of considerable importance, and I can never sufficiently regret not having had it in my power to make them.

It may, perhaps, be doubted whether the globe of iron I have mentioned could be made to penetrate through the tenacious superficies of the lava: but there seems little reason for this doubt, when we consider that the pieces of porous lava, which are far lighter than this metal, penetrated it to one third of their bulk. And though it should not be able to divide that part of the superficies which, by being in contact with the air, has less liquidity; that might be separated by other means, and the globe immediately plunged into the more fluid part of the lava.

I do not deny but that these and other similar experiments are difficult, offensive, and, in some degree, even dangerous; but what experiment can be undertaken perfectly free from inconvenience, and all fear of danger, on mountains which vomit forth fire? I would certainly advise the philosopher who wishes always to make his observations entirely at his ease, and without risk, never to visit volcanoes.

But it is time to continue my narrative of the phenomena I observed in this eruption of Vesuvius. Though the lava issued at its origin from only a narrow aperture, the stream of it became considerably enlarged as it descended the declivity of the mountain, and formed other smaller torrents: but at about the space of a mile from the mouth whence it issued, its superficies had acquired the solidity of stone. I endeavoured to pass over this, notwithstanding the difficulty of walking on it, as it was entirely composed of small disjoined scoriæ, on which the foot could not rest with firmness, and so hot that I was obliged to change my shoes, those I had being worn out, and half-burnt.

Besides

Besides two other pits, similar to that I have described, and some burning orifices in which, when I looked into them, I could perceive the liquid lava resembling melted glass in a furnace when it burns with the utmost violence, I observed, likewise, the traces of the course which the lava had taken or resumed. Here the channels through which it had flowed remained, but empty; there some residue of it was to be seen; and others were full of it. One had the form of a cylindric tube, and another that of a parallelopiped. But the direction of all these channels through which the lava had flowed, was towards the south. It did not require much attention to perceive, that under the solid lava on which I walked the fluid was still running; the low but distinct sound it occasioned in its passage was clearly perceptible to the ear.

A sufficient illustration of what I mean may be given from what frequently happens, in winter, to many slow streams, in the northern parts of Italy. In these, when

the

the winter is severe, the superficies of the water at first adheres to the banks, and afterwards congeals in the middle, forming a crust of ice which increases in thickness, from night to night, while the water, which is still fluid, if there is sufficient depth, continues to run under it; though the thickness of the ice increases, till after some days it is sufficiently strong to bear men to walk on it, or even greater weights. If any person should then go upon it, and apply his ear close to it, he would hear the sound of the water running under, as I have several times experienced in the vicinity of Pavia. This sound appears to me to be precisely the same with that occasioned by the Vesuvian lava flowing under the solid lava, and proceeds doubtless from the same cause; I mean the obstacles the fluids meet with and strike against in their passage; as the cause of congelation is likewise the same in both, that is, the privation or rather the diminution of their absolute heat.

Pursuing my way to the south, along the declivity

declivity of the mountain, I arrived at the part where the lava ran above the ground. Where the stream was broadest, it was twenty-two feet in breadth, and eighteen where narrowest. The length of this torrent was two miles, or nearly so. This stream of lava, when compared with others which have flowed from Vesuvius, and extended to the distance of five or six miles, with a proportionate breadth, must certainly suffer in the comparison; but considered in itself, and especially by a person unaccustomed to such scenes, it cannot but astonish and most powerfully affect the mind. When I travelled in Switzerland, the impression made upon me by the Glacieres was, I confess, great; to see, in the midst of summer, immense mountains of ice and snow, placed on enormous rocks, and to find myself shake with cold, wrapped up in my pelisse on their frozen cliffs, while in the plain below Nature appeared languid with the extreme heat. But much more forcibly was I affected at the sight of this torrent of lava, which resembled a river of fire. It issued

from

from an aperture excavated in the congealed lava, and took its courſe towards the ſouth. For thirty or forty paces from its ſource, it had a red colour, but leſs ardent than that of the lava which flowed within the cavern I have mentioned above. Through this whole ſpace its ſurface was filled with tumours which momentarily aroſe and diſappeared. I was able to approach it to within the diſtance of ten feet; but the heat I felt was extremely great, and almoſt inſupportable, when the air, put in motion, croſſed the lava, and blew upon me. When I threw into the torrent pieces of the hardened lava, they left a very ſlight hollow trace. The ſound they produced was like that of one ſtone ſtriking againſt another; and they ſwam following the motion of the ſtream. The torrent at firſt deſcended down an inclined plain which made an angle of about 45 degrees with the horizon, flowing at the rate of eighteen feet in a minute; but at about the diſtance of thirty or forty paces from its ſource, its ſuperficies, cleared from the tumours I have before mentioned, ſhewed ed only large flakes of the substance of the lava, of an extremely dull red, which, clashing together, produced a confused sound, and were borne along by the current under them.

Observing these phenomena with attention, I perceived the cause of this diversity of appearance. The lava, when it issued from the subterranean caverns, began, from the impression of the cold air, to lose its fluidity, so that it yielded less to the stroke of solid bodies. The loss of this principle, however, was not such as to prevent the superficies from flowing. But at length it diminished by the increasing induration; and then, the superficial part of the lava, by the unequal adhesion of its parts, was separated into flakes, which would have remained motionless had they not been borne away by the subjacent matter, which still remained fluid, on account of its not being exposed to the immediate action of the air, in the same manner as water carries on its surface floating flakes of ice.

Proceeding further, I perceived that the ſtream was covered, not only with theſe flakes, but with a great quantity of ſcoriæ; and the whole maſs of theſe floating matters was carried away by the fluid lava, with unequal velocity, which was ſmall where the declivity was ſlight, but confiderable when it was great. In one place, for ten or twelve feet, the deſcent was ſo ſteep that it differed little from a perpendicular. The lava muſt therefore be expected there to form a cataract. This it, in fact, did, and no fight could be more curious. When it arrived at the brow of this deſcent, it fell headlong, forming a large liquid ſheet of a pale red, which daſhed with a loud noiſe on the ground below, where the torrent continued its courſe as before.

It appeared to me that it might be expected that, where the channel was narrow, the velocity of the torrent muſt be increaſed, and where it was capacious diminiſhed; but I obſerved that, in proportion as it removed from its ſource, its progreſſive motion

tion became flower: and the reason for this is extremely obvious; since the current of melted matter being continually exposed to the cold air, must continually lose some portion of its heat, and, consequently, of its fluidity.

At length the lava, after having continued its course about two miles, along the declivity of the mountain, stopped, and formed a kind of small lake, but solid, at least on the superficies. Here the fiery redness disappeared; but about two hundred feet higher it was still visible, and more apparent still nearer to its source. From the whole of this lake, strong sulphureous fumes arose, which were likewise to be observed at the sides, where the lava had ceased to flow, but still retained a considerable degree of heat.

After having written these observations on the lava ejected by Vesuvius, as it appeared from its source to its termination, which I made in company with Dr. Comi

Abruz-

Abruzzese, a young student of great promise in medical and physical science, I had an opportunity to read the accounts of former eruptions, as they have been given by men of great abilities, who had observed them on the spot, I mean Dr. Serao, Father Della Torre, M. Deluc, and Sir William Hamilton. I perceive that, in the principal facts, the phenomena I have observed agree with their observations, and that the differences are but few. Thus the torrents of lava which they have described were accompanied with great fumes, and covered with pieces of lava and scoriæ. In like manner the liquid lava received but small impressions from the stroke of solid bodies, and sometimes none. Serao informs us, that the lava of 1737, when struck on the surface with long pointed staves, was found to be so hard that it resounded. According to the observation of Father Della Torre, the thick lava of the eruption of 1754, when raised with long poles, split into pieces. M. Deluc shewed me, some years since, in his private cabinet

of

of Natural History, at Geneva, a piece of Vesuvian lava, of the eruption of 1758, marked with a flight impression, which he made on it, on the spot, while it retained its softness. If this naturalist should ever chance to come to Pavia, I could shew him, in return, in the public Imperial Museum, among the collection of volcanic productions which I have made, a cylinder of lava, 18 inches long, and $5\frac{1}{2}$ thick, which, in one part, has been bent to an angle, while it was half liquid, by the hands of the guide who accompanied me when I visited the eruption I have above described. In the eruption of 1766, likewise, though the lava flowed with surprising velocity, we are told, by Sir William Hamilton, that it received but a very slight impression from some large stones that he threw into it. Father Della Torre has also remarked another phenomenon which I observed, and have described, relative to the effervescence and tumours of the fluid lava.

But my meeting with the subterranean cavity in which the lava flowed, was a fortunate

tunate and fingular circumftance, which is not, that I know of, mentioned by any one elfe, becaufe probably it was not feen; fince all the defcriptions of eruptions which we have, relate folely to currents of lava running over the furface of the ground, expofed to the free action of the air; from the effect of which the lava muft foon cool and harden; as appears from the very flight impreffion made by ftones thrown into it, according to all the accounts I have cited, and my own obfervations. But the narrownefs of this cavern, and in fome meafure its depth, prevented this action of the air; whence I was enabled to obferve the lava in a ftate in which it cannot be feen above the ground, ftill retaining a great part of its fluidity, as appeared from its from time to time fpouting into the air, and from the impreffions made on it by the pieces of lava thrown into it. It cannot, therefore, be doubted but it had a much greater degree of fluidity when it boiled up in the Vefuvian furnace; as it muft then have been penetrated with a greater quantity of abfolute heat, by the action of which its

parts

parts muſt have been more disjoined and ſeparated, and therefore have poſſeſſed a greater degree of fluidity and mobility. But I ſhall adduce ſtill ſtronger reaſons to prove the great fluidity of the lava, when it foams and boils up in its craters, when I come to ſpeak of the volcano of Stromboli. I dwell the longer on this ſubject, becauſe I know ſome have denied that the lava is ever fluid, aſſerting, that it has only the conſiſtence of paſte moiſtened with a good deal of water, and deſcends down any declivity in conſequence of its gravity.

To complete the obſervations I have made on this eruption, nothing appears to remain but to ſpeak of the quality of the ejected lava. On this I made different experiments, all of which, ſome extrinſic or accidental circumſtances excepted, furniſhed the ſame reſults. The baſe of the lava is of horn-ſtone rock, of a dark-grey colour, of moderate hardneſs, dry to the touch, where it has been freſh broken ſomewhat earthy, and gives ſome ſparks with the ſteel.

steel. This lava put the magnetic needle in motion at the distance of three lines and a half, or somewhat more than a quarter of an inch.

It is well known to volcanic naturalists, that many of the lavas of Vesuvius contain colourless garnets. In that of which I treat, they were found very numerous, though very small. When broken, they appeared glassy; and sometimes a kind of side or face was visible, though without its being possible to determine the quality of the cryftallization, not so much from their smallness as from their being too intimately incorporated with their tenacious matrix. With the garnets were united a number of shoerls, of the colour and lustre of asphaltum, vitreous, cryftallized in faces, the largest of which was nearly five lines. Those which were found in the running lava had received no injury from the fire; but those in the globes ejected from the crater in that eruption, were in a state of beginning fusion.

The fire of the furnace changed this lava into a kind of enamel, full of bubbles, of the colour of pitch, shining, which gave sparks with steel, and adhered strongly to the sides of the crucible *. The shoerls melted, but the garnets did not; they only became whitish, but without entirely losing their vitreous appearance.

After having made my observations on the phenomena exhibited by the stream of lava then running, I proceeded to examine the vestiges of others which had flowed some time before; one of which, in November 1785, had issued at about one third of a mile from its crater, on the side of

---

* To avoid repetitions, I shall here mention, that, when I use the word *furnace* without any other addition, I always mean the furnace of a glass-house; and that by the term *enamel*, I understand, with the generality of our chemists, a substance produced by heat, resembling glass, but without its transparency. It may also be proper to add, that, as often as an entire fusion of the lava took place in the crucibles, it adhered strongly to the sides.

Monte Somma. As I do not know that any notice has yet been taken of it by others, I shall relate the observations I made as I passed over the remains of it, and likewise the information given me concerning it by my guide, and some persons who cultivate the study of Natural History, who had observed it on the spot at the time of its eruption.

Although at its source it was but narrow (as generally happens to these streams of lava), it afterwards became considerably enlarged, and did not form small, disjoined, and rugged pieces like the others I have described; but large masses, many feet in breadth and depth, and separated by numerous fissures. Its superficies presented an appearance not a little curious. It was rugged and irregular, from an immense number of small cylindric bodies resembling twisted cords, and which were only the lava itself reduced into striated and contorted fibres, when near the end of its course, and ready to congeal. In its qualities it did not appear to me to differ

from

from the other Vesuvian lava I had already examined, either in its base or the garnets and shoerls which it contained.

The greater part of this lava lies in a valley under Massa, and on one side of Salvatore. Before it arrived there, it must have fallen from a high rock, and consequently formed a cataract, which, when seen by night, I was told, exhibited a most wonderful spectacle to the eyes of beholders. But though its fall through the air must have been very considerable, and it must in consequence have lost much of its heat, when it reached the ground it continued still to flow for a considerable space. On the side of Massa, I observed that it had approached within ten or twelve feet of some oaks which grew on the side of a precipice. Some of them appeared entirely withered; others preserved their verdure only on that side of the trunk and branches which was opposite to that next the lava. In its passage it did such damage to a small church called *Madonna della*

della Vetrana, that it has ever since remained deserted. The fiery torrent took it in front, and broke down the wall, which indeed required no great force, as it was built with soft stones of tufa brought from the neighbouring mountains of Massa, and much like that of Naples. Thence it penetrated into the church, and having destroyed the door on the opposite side, and beat down a part of the wall, continued its course, through the church, within which it was observed to flow with greater velocity than the rest of the surrounding lava, from being confined by the walls on the sides. With this lava the floor of the edifice still continues covered, and the contiguous sacristy partly filled; while large pieces of the broken wall, which the torrent had carried away, lie at more than eighty feet distance from the church, in the middle of the hardened lava.— Some linden trees are likewise to be seen surrounded by the same, the trunks of which are blackened and burnt. The lava, as I was assured, continued to flow fifteen months;

and

and when I vifited the place, which was ten months after it had ceafed to flow, it was ftill warm, and emitted thin fumes.

On one fide of Vefuvius, about a mile below Salvatore, is a fpacious cavern, which widens as we defcend into it, called the *Foffa Grande*. I took this way to return to Naples, and gained from it confiderable and ufeful information. It is well known what doubts have been entertained relative to the fhoerls and feltfpars which are ufually found, either conjointly or feparately, in the lavas; I mean whether they have been formed within them, either while they were fluid, or at the time of their congelation; or whether they exifted in the original rock before the fire changed it into lava. Bergman has ftated the arguments on each fide, but has left the controverfy undecided. It is true, that, when that chemift wrote on volcanic productions, the opinion was, with good reafon, moft prevalent, which fuppofes that the fhoerls and feltfpars exifted originally in the primordial rocks. This hypothefis has

has received considerable support from the pieces of rock anciently thrown out of Vesuvius, which are to be found on the surface of the ground; or by searching and digging in the tufaceous matters of the *Fossa Grande*.

But it is necessary to proceed to particulars. One species of these rocks is of a margaceous nature, the carbonate of lime however prevailing. As this did not appear to be at all calcined, but unchanged, and similar to stones of the same kind which are not volcanic, it afforded a convincing proof that these rocks have received no sensible injury from the fire; but if we break some of these, we shall find in them numbers of feltspars, which, in their cryftallization, and other exterior characters, extremely refemble many of those we meet with in some lavas of Vesuvius, and other neighbouring volcanic places. Still more numerous also are the shoerls of a shining black; some of the shape of needles, and others of prisms, and varying in their size; some being so small as to be scarcely visible, and others of the

the length of feven lines, or above half an inch, and broad in proportion. Thefe pieces of rock do not form veins, ftrata, or great maffes, but are diftributed in different places in fcattered fragments.

Here likewife we find various pieces of granite, not in the leaft injured by the fire; the quartz of which, befides mica, is accompanied by feltfpars and fhoerls, which in no refpect differ from the volcanic fhoerls and feltfpars.

I might have confiderably extended thefe remarks on the fpecies of rock thrown out by the Vefuvian fires without receiving injury or change; but I think that what I have faid will be fufficient to fhew, that, in order to account for the prefence of feltfpars and fhoerls, in lava, and their various cryftallizations, it is not neceffary to fuppofe them formed within it, either when it was fluid, or at the time of its congelation; fince we meet with fimilar vitreous bodies in the fubftances from which it derives its origin.

CHAP. II.

THE GROTTO OF POSILIPO—SOLFATARA —THE PISCIARELLI.

The city of Naples founded on volcanic substances—Different opinions relative to the origin of volcanic tufas—Those of Posilipo appear to have been formed by thick eruptions—Lavas on the road to Solfatara described—Specular iron found in one of these—Solfatara is not an isolated mountain, as has been supposed by some—Sulphures of iron (or Pyrites) lavas of Solfatara, and the Pisciarelli—Observations on the decomposition of lava, and the shoerls and feltspars which are found within it; as also on the sulphureous-acid fumes which incessantly exhale from this volcano—Conjecture that Solfatara has arisen out of the sea—Method lately employed to extract, more abundantly than formerly, alum and sal ammoniac from this volcano—Critical disquisition relative

relative to a curious phenomenon in the vicinity of Solfatara, from which M Ferber conjectures that the level of the sea has, there, sunk nine feet.

DURING my stay at Naples, I determined to visit the other principal Phlegrean fields as well as Vesuvius, and I had the good fortune to meet with, and have for a companion, the Abbé Breiflak, formerly Professor of Philosophy at Rome, and of Mathematics in the Nazarene College; and now Director of Solfatara, near Pozzuolo.

The beautiful city of Naples is entirely founded on volcanic substances. Among these the tufa predominates, which has also contributed not a little to the materials of many buildings. To the north and west it is accumulated in large heaps, and forms spacious hills. A philosophical stranger, on his arrival in this country, when he views these immense masses of a substance which must excite in his mind the idea of fire, cannot but feel astonishment, and enquire

with

with a kind of serious thoughtfulness, what has been their origin. It is known that on this subject naturalists are divided. Some conjecture that the volcanic tufa was generated within the sea when it bathed the foot of the burning mountains; others suppose that the cinders ejected by the fire, have, in a long course of years, been hardened into this species of stone by the filtration of rain water; lastly, others incline to think that the tufa derives its origin from the slimy and fluid substances thrown out by the volcanos in some of their eruptions.

The diversity of volcanic tufas has, perhaps, been the cause of these different opinions, each of which may, possibly, be true with respect to different kinds of tufa. Those, however, which are found in the vicinity of Naples are, probably, the produce of thick eruptions, as we may conclude from the curious discovery of Sir William Hamilton, who, in digging up, in the tufa which had covered Herculaneum, the head of an antique statue, observed that the perfect impression

pression of the head was visible in the tufa, which cannot be supposed to have happened but by its having enveloped the statue in a liquid or moist state.

To the observation of Sir William let me be permitted to add one of my own, which I made in the grotto of Posilipo. It is well known that this grotto has been excavated within the tufa, and serves as a public road from Naples to Pozzuolo. This tufa, which is of a clear grey, has for its base an earth in part argillaceous, of a slight hardness, which contains vitreous flakes, pieces of feltspars and fragments of yellowish pumice-stone, which by the changes it has undergone has become extremely friable, and almost reducible to powder. This tufa has been in some measure analysed by the excavation made in it by art, which furnishes a proof of the nature of its origin. For if any person, in the summer time, enters the grotto about the rising of the sun, since at other times of the day there is not sufficient light; the solar rays, shining on the entrance which looks towards Naples, will sufficiently illuminate

minate the roof and sides to shew layers or flakes, similar to those which may be observed on the steep sides of mountains, or in perpendicular sections of the earth, in low places, where sediments of various kinds of slime have been formed by the inundations of rivers. It seems, however, impossible to doubt, that this accumulation of tufa, through the midst of which the Romans opened that long and spacious grotto, has been produced by the thick eruptions which have frequently issued from volcanoes, and which, heaping up one upon another, have hardened in time into this tufaceous stone; since both Vesuvius and Etna furnish sufficient examples of such eruptions. And as in many other tufas in the vicinity I have observed a similar constructure; I cannot suppose their origin to have been different.

Coming out of this subterraneous passage, and proceeding towards Solfatara, I observed, on the right hand side of the road, a ridge of lava, nearly parallel with it, which had every appearance of having been thrown out of the

the volcano when burning, both because it was extremely near to it, and had its highest part in that direction. Its thickness exceeded five-and-thirty feet, and it was situated between two layers of tufa, one above and the other below. It formed a high rock, perpendicular to one side of the road. A number of labourers were continually employed in separating pieces of this lava, with pickaxes, or other instruments proper for such work. It is compact, heavy, somewhat vitreous, gives sparks with steel, and appeared to me to have for its base the petrosilex. Incorporated with it are found shoerls and feltspars. The former are shining, of a dark violet-colour, in shape rectangular needles, vitreous, in length, from the sixth of a line to two lines: it besides contains a considerable quantity of others which have no regular form. But the feltspars are more conspicuous than the shoerls; both from their larger size and greater number. They are, in general, of a flat rhomboidal form, and consist of an aggregate of small white lamellæ, dully transparent, brilliant,

liant, marked with longitudinal ſtreaks parallel to each other, cloſely adhering together, but eaſily ſeparated by the hammer, giving ſparks with ſteel more readily than the lava; and, in the full light of day, exhibiting that changing colour which uſually accompanies this ſtone. The largeſt are ten lines long and ſix broad, and the ſmalleſt exceed one line. The ſhoerls are alſo found in the lava, in the ſame manner, and are ſo fixed in it, that they occupy nearly the half of it. It is impoſſible to extricate them entire. They are diſtributed within it without any order, and frequently croſs and interſect each other at right angles.

In ſome ſituations of this lava, which are more than others expoſed to the inclemency of the air and ſeaſons, the feltſpars are viſible on the ſuperficies, by a mixture of emerald and paonazzo, probably occaſioned by the action of the atmoſphere, as from the ſame cauſe ſome volcanic vitrifactions acquire externally their peculiar colour.

This lava has not equal folidity throughout, being in fome places porous, or rather cavernous; and, in fome of its varieties, it was remarkable, that it abounded with fpecular iron. This was found in very thin leaves, for the moft part, clofely connected together. Thefe are extremely friable; and the finger being paffed over them, they adhere to it like particles of mica. But their fmall fize, which, in the largeft, is fcarcely a line, renders it neceffary to make ufe of a lens to examine them properly; by the aid of which we fhall find that they are of very different fhapes, have the luftre of burnifhed fteel, and that many of them appear to be an aggregate of fmall thin fcales, clofely united.

This iron acts on the magnetic needle, at the diftance of two lines. Like many other irons expofed to the air, it has acquired polarity; attracting the needle, on one fide, and repelling it on the other.

When we extract thefe thin fcales of iron from the lava, and examine them with
the

the lens, there frequently appear, intermingled with them, various fragments of microscopic transparent prisms, which I, at first, thought to be shoerls, or feltspars; but which, afterwards, I rather conceived to be zeolites, as they exhibited the appearance of radii diverging from a centre: but their extreme minuteness rendered it impossible accurately to ascertain their species.

Proceeding along the road to Solfatara, we find, on the left hand, a natural ridge of rock, formed of a very light lava, the base of which is horn-stone, of the colour of blue baked brick, of a coarse earthy grain, which attaches slightly to the tongue, and gives an argillaceous scent, on wetting it, or even merely moistening it with the breath *.

---

* In many lavas, the scent of clay is perceived, on moistening them with the breath, or by other means: whenever, therefore, I may, hereafter, mention the argillaceous scent of lava; I always understand it to have been subjected to this humectation, though I omit to mention it, to avoid prolixity.

It is very probable that this lava has been decompofed, and that the decompofition has penetrated to the feltfpars with which it abounds, as they are become very friable, though they in general ftill retain their natural brilliancy.

Having made thefe curfory obfervations, I proceeded to Solfatara: nor did I fatisfy myfelf with one vifit only, but repeated it feveral days; being extremely defirous carefully to examine, and gain every information relative to a place fo celebrated.

From reading the notes of M. Dietrich to Ferber's Travels in Italy; I had been induced to imagine that Solfatara was a mountain ifolated on every fide*; but the truth is, it is connected with the other neighbouring mountains, with which it forms an uninterrupted chain of confiderable extent.

---

* La Solfatare repréfente encore aujourd'hui une montagne affez élevée et ifolée de tous côtés.—*Lettres fur la Minéralogie*, &c. *de l'Italie*, &c.

It would be but of little utility for me to defcribe, at length, the form, extent, and circuit of this Phlegrean field; the various qualities of the hot vapours which exhale from it; or the hollow noife which is heard on ftriking the ground in various parts of it; not that thefe circumftances were not carefully examined by me; or that I think them unworthy of my narrative; but becaufe it appears to me unneceffary to enlarge on them; as they have been already repeatedly defcribed by a great number of travellers. It will, in my opinion, be more agreeable to the naturalift to proceed to a minute examination of the principal productions of this yet unextinguifhed volcano, as they have hitherto been, for the moft part, either unobferved, or paffed over in filence.

In the obfcurity and uncertainty in which we find ourfelves, relative to the caufes productive of fubterraneous conflagrations, the fpontaneous inflammation of fulphures of iron (or pyrites) has been confidered as one of the moft probable. The well-known experiment of Lemery, by which a similar conflagration is produced by mixing filings of iron with powdered sulphur properly moistened, has given great support to this opinion. But sulphures of iron, in volcanic countries, are less frequent than has been supposed. This has been clearly proved by the accurate observations of mineralogists who have written on them. And though Sir William Hamilton expressly affirms that both Etna and Vesuvius abound with them *, it is now well known that he mistook the shoerls for sulphures of iron (or pyrites), from want of mineralogical knowledge. In fact, Signior Dolomieu, in his *Catologo Ragionato de' Prodotti dell' Etna*, mentions only one single piece of lava as containing sulphure of iron: and the Chevalier Gioeni, in his *Litologia Vesuviana*, has never noticed any such production. In Volcano and Stromboli, two islands which are in a state of actual conflagration, I could trace no vestiges of such sulphures, as will be remarked in the proper place. As the same kind of

---

* Both these mountains abound with pyrites.
Campi Phlegræi.

substance, therefore, is found diffused in several parts of Solfatara, I think it well deserves that we should carefully consider it, and the bodies with which it is found united.

I. The stones which I here undertake to describe are principally found in the interior sides of Solfatara. The first I shall mention exhibits, both externally and internally, a number of shining particles, which, when examined by the lens, appear to be small aggregates of sulphure of iron, some crystallized in cubes, others in globes, and others in irregular figures. When the flame of the blow-pipe is applied to them, they begin to lose their yellow colour, which, quickly, in consequence of their destruction, entirely disappears; when an odour slightly sulphureous is emitted.

This substance is a lava, the base of which is horn-stone; in part decomposed, light, friable, granulous, and of a cinereous colour.

II. The small sulphures of iron in this second

cond lava are lefs numerous, but in their qualities very analogous to that already defcribed; except that they are lefs decompofed, and lefs friable.

III. The appearances exhibited by this lava are two. The external part is extremely white; and fo decompofed, that the flighteft blow reduces it to powder; we likewife find in it fome of the external characters of ordinary clay. It tenacioufly adheres to the infide of the lip; is foft to the touch, and becomes ftill more fo when flightly moiftened. It abforbs water greedily, and with a kind of hiffing noife; but is not reducible to a lubricious pafte, as clay is. But the internal part of this lava, befides being of a grey colour, is three fourths heavier, and in its compactnefs, and its grain, approaches to that fpecies of calcareous earth, called *calcareus æquabilis*, though, in fact, it only refembles it in appearance, not being reduced to calx by fire, nor diffolved by acids. In this lava, the fulphure of iron is not found in cubes, or globes, but in thin lamellæ; and is difperfed throughout its whole fubftance, efpecially in certain parts, where the colour of the ftone inclines to black, and has a greater confiftency. No fign of this mineral appears in the white decompounded lava, probably becaufe it was deftroyed gradually, in proportion as the decompofition took place.

IV. This lava is much heavier than the three preceding; which, no doubt, arifes from the greater abundance of fulphure of iron that it contains. The fhining particles of this mineral are principally to be feen in its vacuities (of which, however, it has not many). They are polyhedrous, but the number of their faces is not conftant. When expofed to the fire it lofes its braffy colour, burns with a thin blue flame, and emits a ftrong fmell of fulphur. The lava which contains it, and which is of a livid grey colour, is, in fome fituations, fo foft that it may be fcratched with the nail, but in others much harder, and fome of it will give fparks with fteel. In this lava, the bafe of which
appeared

appeared to me to be horn-ftone, we find cryf- tallized feltfpars, but decompofed, though lefs fo than the lava in which they are in- clofed.

V. Around the extenfive plain of Solfa- tara, we obferve, in feveral places, a circular ridge of fteep rocks, which once formed the upper fides of this enormous crater. The rain water, defcending this declivity, over the decompofed lava, carries down with it the more minute parts to the lower grounds, where various concretions are produced, efpecially thofe ftalactites which are commonly called *oolithes*, or *pifolithes*. But of thefe ftalactites we fhall fpeak here- after. Here we fhall only notice, that this water, in its defcent, carries down with it fmall pieces of decompofed lava, and that, in fome places, many of thefe pieces are found united, and bound together by a cruft of fulphure of iron. It is black where it is expofed to the immediate action of the air, but, in the fractures of a fhining appearance, though the colour inclines more to a lead-colour than to yellow. Its ſtructure is ſcaly. The ſulphures of iron which have before been mentioned give fire with ſteel; but this does not, from want of ſufficient hardneſs. It abounds with ſulphur; ſince, being expoſed to the flame of the blow-pipe, it viſibly melts, and, the activity of the fire being increaſed, a blue flame ariſes, which continues till the cruſt is conſumed, nothing remaining but a very ſmall quantity of a white pulverous earth, which is no other than a portion of decompoſed lava, that had been united with this ſulphur.

With this ſulphur, the preſence of which is extremely manifeſt from its ſtrong ſmell, is alſo united arſenic; as ſufficiently appears from the white fumes which ariſe from the combuſtion of the ſulphure of iron, and which emit a very ſenſible odour of garlic.

Theſe are the volcanic matters which, at Solfatara, abound more or leſs with ſulphures of iron. But whence is their origin? It is well known they are formed by the combination

nation of fulphur with iron. With the former this volcano abounds, whence it obtained the name of Solfatara; and, as the latter is almoſt always found mixed with volcanic productions, which commonly derive from it their varying colours, we have thus the two proximate principles of fulphure of iron. But is their combination effected by the dry, or, as is more probable, by the humid way? I find it difficult to conceive how it can take place by the firſt method, on account of the ſpeedy diſſipation of the fulphur ſublimed by fire, which muſt prevent its uniting with the iron to form theſe fulphures. It appears to me more probable that they have been formed by the action of water, which having penetrated the lava, the fulphur, diſſolving in the fluid, has combined with the iron. But as ſuch ſolutions of fulphur in water ſeldom take place, as Bergman has obſerved, we rarely find fulphures of iron, in volcanized countries, notwithſtanding the exiſtence of theſe two minerals.

But

But let us continue the defcription of the productions of this celebrated place, the greater part of which are decompofed lavas; though this decompofition, notwithftanding it has been noticed by feveral writers, has not, to my knowledge, been examined, by any one, with requifite care and attention.

VI. This lava is coloured on the upper part with a covering of oxyde of yellow iron, under which is a white decompofed ftratum, to which correfponds another lower one of a cinereous colour, where the lava is much lefs changed. Thefe two ftrata form a very ftrong contraft. The white may be cut with a knife, in fome places more eafily and in fome lefs; adheres to the tongue, does not give fparks with fteel, feels foft to the wet finger paffed over it, has confiderable lightnefs, and being ftruck with a hammer gives a dull found, like earth moderately hardened. On the contrary the cinereous ftratum founds, when ftruck with a hammer, like a hard ftone, of which it alfo

has

has the weight; is rough to the touch, scarcely at all adheres to the tongue, gives fire with steel, and cannot be cut with the knife. The white stratum, in some places, is an inch thick, and in others more, but there are likewise places where it is only a few lines in thickness. The white stratum, in general, changes insensibly into the cinereous, but in some places the separation is sudden and abrupt.

The feltspars in this lava (for of these it is full) are prisms; the largest of which are ten lines in length, and the smallest the sixth of a line. In the cinereous stratum, notwithstanding a beginning decomposition may be perceived, the feltspars are unimpaired. On the contrary, in the more decomposed stratum, I mean the white, their decomposition is very apparent; they have all lost their transparency, though many of them still retain their splendour. Others have acquired a resemblance to a sulphate of lime that has remained some time in the fire; to which they might likewise be compared in softness, had they a little less consistence. Some of them are

are infixed in that part of the lava, the colour of which is between the cinereous and white, and here we find them lefs changed than in the ftratum which is entirely white. Others have one part of them in the white, and the other in the cinereous ftratum; in which cafe we find the part fixed in the latter ftratum to have fuffered nothing, but that in the former confiderably. In fhort, from the infpection of this lava, it is manifeft, that, in proportion as the nature of it is changed, the feltfpars it contains undergo a change, except when the principle producing the alteration is unable to affect them. Befides thefe feltfpars, we find, incorporated with the lava, a number of very fmall, and almoft invifible, black fhoerls; which are not diftinguifhable where the lava is white; lefs, perhaps, becaufe they do not exift, than becaufe they have loft their colour, in confequence of the decompofition.

This lava, which is of a margaceous bafe, does not liquefy in the furnace, when its decompofition is confiderable; but other parts of it, which have been lefs decompofed, are reduced to a kind of frit.

VII. Solfatara, perhaps, does not afford a lava more compact, hard, heavy, or of finer grain than this. Its compofition is filiceous, its colour grey, it gives fparks ftrongly with fteel, and, at the diftance of two lines, attracts the magnetic needle. Its bafe is of the petrofilex, and it contains within it different feltfpars and fhoerls; but fome of the latter have been melted by the fire, as appears from the bubbles or fpeckles occafioned by the liquefaction. This lava is covered with a very white cruft, nearly an inch thick, produced by the decompofition it has undergone. The effects of the furnace on this lava, are nearly the fame with thofe on the lava N° VI.

VIII. This lava is entirely decompofed. On the furface, and for fome depth, it is white, and almoft pulverous; but in the internal part the white colour changes into a reddifh blue, and acquires a degree of hardnefs; though not too great to be cut with a knife. The feltfpars, in which it abounds, have fuffered different degrees of
decom-

decomposition. Some of them, besides being calcined, attach strongly to the tongue. Others, when viewed with a common lens, appear full of filaments; but when examined with a deeper magnifier, these filaments appear to be no other than extremely thin, striated, and very friable laminæ. This production is infusible in the furnace.

IX. The feltspars, in this lava, occupy more than one third of its mass. They are in shape flat prisms, and, except having somewhat less hardness, retain all the qualities which characterize the species of stone to which they belong. There are also a number of shoerls, which, from their extreme minuteness, appear like points, but are easily distinguishable, by their black colour, from the lava, which is whitish, and has greater consistence than that of N° VIII. It is likewise heavier; to which the quantity of feltspars but little changed, which it contains, undoubtedly contributes.

X. The shoerls which make so great a part

part of the other kinds of lava, are found fo ftrongly adherent to them, that we ufually can only feparate them in fragments. The prefent lava, in this refpect, offers an exception which may be confidered as recommendatory of it. It has acquired fo great a degree of foftnefs by its decompofition, that the numerous fhoerls it contains may be detached from it entire. They are hexagonal prifms, truncated perpendicular to their axes, the faces of which are flightly ftriated lengthwife, and their colour is a yellowifh black.

In this lava, the bafe of which appeared to me of horn-ftone, another more remarkable peculiarity prefents itfelf. On breaking it, the fractures difcover a number of fmall caverns, jewelled, if I may employ the term, with a multitude of extremely minute fhoerls, of different colours, fome green, fome yellow, others of a dark chefnut, but all fimilar, being hexagonal prifms, with rhomboidal faces, and each terminating in a dihedrous pyramid. Their

angles

angles are regular, their faces fhining, and in part tranfparent. They fometimes form geodes in the body of the lava. To examine them a lens is neceffary, and a good magnifier clearly to perceive other fhoerls ftill more minute. Thefe are infixed in the fmall cavities I before mentioned, and, though they are extended to a confiderable length in front of the others before defcribed, are fo minute and numerous, that a fingle cavity will contain a hundred of them. Every one of both thefe kinds of fhoerls has one extremity fixed in the lava, and the other in the air, and all together appear like a wood in miniature. I was, at firft, in doubt whether I fhould confider them as fhoerls or volcanic glafs, as more than one inftance has been known of fuch glafs reduced to a capillary minutenefs within lava. But the latter appeared to me improbable, becaufe, after all the obfervations that have hitherto been made, we are not yet certain that any volcanic glafs has been found cryftallized; for, with refpect to the pretended cryftallization of fome glaffes in Iceland,

Iceland, we have not facts which demonstrate it incontrovertibly. On the other hand, the minute corpuscles I have described, if not all, at least those which from their larger size are more discernible by the eye, have a prismatic figure, and analogy must induce us to conclude the same of the rest.

I incline to believe these infinitesimal crystallizations produced, after the cooling of the lava, within the cavity in which they are found, from extremely subtle shoerlaceous sediments, by the filtration of water. But we shall have occasion to speak of similar adventitious crystallizations within the substance of lava, in another part of this work.

XI. The *Oolites*, mentioned in No. V. lie in certain small channels of Solfatara, through which the water runs when it rains. They are either round, or somewhat flattened; rather more than half an inch in diameter, white as snow, extremely light, easily crumbled, and convertible into an almoſt impalpable powder. They adhere ſtrongly to the tongue, and are compoſed of a number of thin ſcales. The formation, therefore, of this volcanic ſtalactites does not differ from that of the other ſpecies.

It would be ſuperfluous to ſpeak here of the ſulphate of lime, adhering to ſome kinds of lava, or of the ſulphate of iron, and the oxyde of red ſulphurate arſenic, as theſe productions of Solfatara have already been ſufficiently examined and deſcribed by others, and I have no particular obſervations concerning them which merit to be mentioned.

XII. It is not uncommon to find at Solfatara pumices of various ſpecies; and it is more probable that they have been thrown out of this volcano than from any of the others. We do not find them in great maſſes, as in other places, but in detached pieces and fragments. I ſhall only remark one particular relative to them, as it appears to me that in every other reſpect they perfectly reſemble thoſe already known. We
now

now know that pumice is only a glafs which wants but little of being perfect; and feems to require only a degree more of heat to become fuch. The tranfition from glafs lefs perfect to perfect, may be perceived in fome of thefe pumices in a very evident manner. In fome places their texture is fibrous, and the fibres are vitreous; but without that fmoothnefs, that luftre, and that degree of tranfparency, which are infeparable from volcanic glaffes. But, following them with the eye, we perceive them confolidate, here and there, into maffes of various fizes, which refemble a fhining and fmooth varnifh, but are in fact perfect glafs, as will fufficiently appear, if they be detached from the pumice, and examined feparately. Thefe are fufficiently hard to give fparks with fteel, a property obfervable in every volcanic glafs.

Having now defcribed the principal productions of the interior part of Solfatara, I fhall proceed to make a few obfervations on fome which are found in its exterior; in that part which is next to the Pifciarelli, fo called from the warm bubbling water, which iffues,

iffues, with fome noife, from the bottom of a little hill contiguous to this volcano, and which has been long celebrated for its medicinal virtues. I collected here specimens of five kinds of lava; but, as in their general qualities they are analogous to thofe already defcribed, I fhall only mention them in a curfory manner.

XIII. The firft fpecimen is a fimple or homogeneous lava, in which, notwithftanding the moft careful examination, I could not difcover either fhoerls, feltfpars, or any extraneous body. In other refpects, like thofe before mentioned, it is decompofed, adheres to the tongue, is friable, but without crumbling under the finger; its whitenefs extends through its whole mafs, and whereever it is broken has the tafte of fulphate of alumine, (or alum).

XIV. The fecond fpecimen, through nearly the half of it, exhibits a fimilar decompofition, and is of a white colour; but the other half, which is of a lead colour,

has

has fuffered little, gives fparks ftrongly with fteel, and moves the magnetic needle at two lines diftance. This lava has for its bafe the petrofilex. Both that part of it which is flightly decompofed, and the other which is more fo, contain rhomboidal feltfpars, of which the largeft are about an inch in length. Their alteration is fcarcely vifible where the lava is leaft changed; and where it is more they exfoliate with fome facility, but retain a confiderable degree of their natural hardnefs and fplendour.

XV. The third fpecimen is a lava of a dark grey colour, filiceous where fractured, very compact, and which gives fparks with fteel. It is of a petrofiliceous bafe, and contains abundance of feltfpars and fhoerls. But to fhew thefe, it is neceffary to diveft it of a thick, whitifh, and half-pulverous cruft, produced by its decompofition. In this cruft the fhoerls and feltfpars retain fome confiftence, but have loft, in a great degree, their luftre.

XVI. The fourth specimen contains within it a nucleus of a deep red colour, of the hardness and appearance of the carbonates of lime (calcareous earths), of a fine grain, but which is not dissolved or affected by acids, nor yields sparks with steel. It attracts the magnetic needle at the distance of one line. It contains a number of fissures, through which has penetrated, together with water, a quartzous matter, which has consolidated into a semi-transparent, and somewhat rough, covering. In this lava, which is but little decomposed, are found, dispersed, a number of small masses of sulphure of iron.

XVII. Small shoerls, and large crystallized feltspars, occupy the substance of this last lava, which is somewhat porous, but sufficiently hard to give sparks with steel. It is covered with a whitish-yellow crust, which flakes off with a knife, and a reddish tincture has penetrated to its internal part, which is of a blackish ground.

In thefe lavas of Pifciarelli, the decompofition has, likewife, been much more confiderable, than in the feltfpars and fhoerls which they contain within them.

I do not pretend to be certain that I have enumerated all the fpecies of lava to be found at Solfatara: it is poffible there may be others unobferved by me. I am perfuaded, however, that I have defcribed the principal; and fuch as enable me to deduce from their qualities the following conclufions.

I.

Almoft all the fpecies of lava hitherto defcribed, are more or lefs decompofed, and this decompofition is ufually accompanied with a proportionable degree of whitenefs. This obfervation has been made by feveral authors; and firft by Sir William Hamilton, and M. Ferber, who have endeavoured to account for the fact by a very plaufible reafon, which is, that the fulphureous-acid vapours, which iffue from Solfatara, and muft have

have been produced in an infinitely greater quantity, when the conflagration was at its height, penetrating the lava by degrees, have infenfibly foftened it, and given it a white colour. And, in fact, fimilar changes are obferved to take place in a piece of black lava, expofed for a fufficient time to the fumes of burning fulphur. But it does not hence follow that this lava will be changed into an argillaceous fubftance, as the above-mentioned Swedifh philofopher would have us believe; fince, from a chemical analyfis, it appears that an earth of that kind, combined with other principles, pre-exifted in it, and has only been rendered manifeft by the diminution of aggregation produced by the before-mentioned vapours.

It is likewife not ftrictly true that the walls, or inclofing fides, of Solfatara are every where white and decompofed, as we might infer from the defcription of M. Ferber. Thofe which look toward the fouth, indeed, are fo, but not thofe which are fituated in another direction, and efpecially
thofe

those which front the north, which are of a blackish colour, and little, or not at all, decomposed. The Abbé Breislak, Director of Solfatara, who accompanied me when I made my observations, suggested a very probable reason for this diversity of appearance in the different sides, observing that the sulphureous acid is less powerful to effect the decomposition of lava, and requires longer time, when the lava has considerable humidity; which humidity must be much less on the southern side, where the heat of the sun is greatest. In fact, he exposed a piece of solid lava, to a very humid sulphureous exhalation, at Solfatara, during two months, without producing in it the least decomposition.

II.

The observations I have made, convince me that the alterations here described always take place in the upper part of the lava; and that, in proportion as we penetrate downwards into it, they become gradually less, and, at a certain depth, entirely cease. This, at firſt view, does not appear to accord with the effect of ſulphureous vapours, which, riſing from the bottom of Solfatara, and paſſing through the lava, might be expected to cauſe a greater change in the lower parts than the higher, from their having there greater heat, and conſequently being more active. But we muſt conſider that this may indeed be the nature of their action, where the lava is ſpongy, or at leaſt very porous, but not where it is compact, and almoſt impenetrable to ſuch vapours; as is that of Solfatara. And, in fact, we find that the ſulphureous fumes which ariſe there, do not iſſue from the body of the lava, but always from fiſſures or apertures in it, or the ſubjacent tufa. Theſe impediments, therefore, prevent them from acting except on the ſurface, when, iſſuing forth, they are driven over it by the wind, and, penetrating the lava, in a long courſe of time, produce the changes in queſtion. We meet with few decompoſed lavas, within which we do not find fragments of ſulphur adherent, condenſed there by the acids above mentioned,

and

and which are of the fame kind with that produced in fuch abundance in Solfatara.

But what productive caufe fhall we affign for thofe fulphureous vapours, the flow deftroyers of the lava, which continually iffue from a number of fiflures in Solfatara, in the form of hot white fumes? I can conceive no principle to which they can with greater probability be afcribed than thofe fulphures of iron, (pyrites), which abound at the bottom of the volcano, and decompofing, in confequence of a mixture with the fubterraneous waters, flowly inflame, and produce thofe hot fulphureous vapours, which evidently prove that the fubterraneous conflagration is not entirely extinguifhed. The noify effervefcence, likewife which, in more than one place is heard under the plain of Solfatara, feems to give a certain indication of the decompofition of thefe fulphures.

The ftreams of vapour, which arife from Solfatara, according to Father Della Torre [*],

[*] Storia del Vefuvio.

in the night, appear like flame. No perfon can be more competent to afcertain the truth of this fact than the Abbé Breiflak, who refides near the place, and who, when I queftioned him on the fubject, affured me that he had never obferved any fuch appearance. It is, however, not impoffible, but that, at the time he obferved them, they might have undergone fome change.

The vapours which arife from the ground of the Pifciarelli are very few, and almoft infenfible, though formerly they muft have been numerous and ftrong, as may be inferred from the great decompofition and whitenefs of the lavas found there. I have already mentioned the noife with which the fprings that bear this name burft from the earth. They refemble a boiling caldron. The reafons affigned for this phenomenon, by different authors, are various, but, hitherto, all conjectural. On applying the ear to the place where the fpring iffues, we may perceive that the bubbling noife does not proceed from any great depth, but from a fmall diftance from the furface of the

the earth. Were the ground, here, to be dug into, we might, perhaps, be able to discover this secret, the knowledge of which might prove advantageous to volcanic researches. My want of time, and other causes, did not permit me to make the experiment myself, when I was at Naples; but I entertain a hope that what I have said may induce some of the lovers of natural knowledge in that city to engage in this undertaking, which I incline to think will not be found useless.

III.

We have seen that almost all the lavas of Solfatara contain within them shoerls and feltspars. But it has been proved that the changes occasioned in both the latter, by the action of sulphureous acids, are considerably less than those which take place in the lavas their matrices; which difference must arise from the nature of these two stones, which is less liable to extrinsic injuries. We find them, in fact, firmly resist the power of the humid elements. To the

the south of Vesuvius, and at a little distance from Salvatore, I have found several pieces of very ancient lava, porous, and half-consumed by time, which, however, preserved unaltered their black crystallized shoerls.

It has been observed that the houses of Pompeii, long since overwhelmed by Vesuvius, and now, in part, dug into, and cleared, are found to have been built of lava. I have ascertained this fact on the spot. They are of a reddish colour, very dry to the touch, and some of them will crumble under the finger, evident proofs of the change they have undergone; but no such alteration has taken place in the shoerls they contain; they still retain the hardness and glassy splendour which is appropriate to that stone.

We likewise know that the feltspars are indestructible by the air, as appears in the porphyries of which they are a part.

IV.

I have already remarked that the lavas of
Solfatara

Solfatara usually have for their basis the petrosilex and the horn-stone. I shall add that I have also met with the granite in them, though not in a large mass, but in small detached pieces, which induced me to doubt whether they properly belong to this volcano; and as they likewise appeared to me untouched by the fire, I rather inclined to believe them adventitious. This granite consists of two substances, quartz and shoerl.

But another production must not be forgotten, which forms large heaps on one side of the internal crater of this volcano. This is an ash-coloured tufa, of a middling consistence, in strata of various thickness, with the superficies of each stratum covered with a black crust, in which may be discovered manifest vestiges of plants. The Abbé Breislak, who first observed this tufa, after having shewn it me on the spot, gave me some of these impressions of plants to examine, conjecturing them to be some species of the *alga marina,* or, sea-weed. While I was at Naples, I had not sufficient time to
make

make an accurate examination of them; but this I afterwards made at Pavia, from several specimens of the same tufa. Some parts exhibited only the impressions of plants, but in others I found real leaves. They are striated, with striæ running lengthwise, and, when touched with the point of a needle, easily break, and appear converted into a carbonaceous substance. At first I doubted whether they were plants of the alga; but, on examining them again, carefully, with a lens, and comparing the leaves found in the tufa with those of the natural alga, I was fully convinced they were.

This observation appeared, both to me and the Abbé Breislak, to be of considerable importance; since we may conclude from it, that the part of Solfatara which is formed by this tufa, has once made a part of the bottom of the sea, and been thrown up by the action of submarine fires. Nor is it improbable that the rest of it has had the same origin, and that all the substances of this volcano have issued from the waters of the sea.

sea. Such we know to have been the origin of many other mountains, either now actually burning, or which have ceased to burn.

It is well known that, for a long time, alum and sal-ammoniac have been extracted from this half-extinguished volcano. The method employed for each was as follows. In the process for the alum, certain square places were cleared out in the plain of Solfatara, in which it effloresced, and the efflorescences were swept together, and, from them, by methods well known, the salt was collected purified. The sal-ammoniac was obtained by placing a number of pieces of tile round the apertures from which that salt issued, in the form of a subtle vapour, upon which the vapour was condensed. A description of these two methods is to be found in almost all the authors who have written on Solfatara; some of whom, with reason, censure them as imperfect, and, consequently, not likely to produce the profit which might be obtained.

But we may now hope that both thefe manufactures may become objects of importance, under the direction of the Abbé Breiflak, and the liberal patronage of Baron Don Giufeppe Brentano, who has taken this celebrated Phlegrean field at a conftant rent. The Abbé, proceeding on the principle that the quantity of alum procured from Solfatara muft be proportionate to the area of the fpace on which it efflorefces, inftead of the narrow fquares, formerly appropriated to this purpofe, and called *gardens*, has greatly extended the fpaces allotted; and that the preparation of this falt may not be prevented, by the rain-water draining into the bottom from the fteep fides of the volcano, he has furrounded them with fmall ditches, with deep wells at intervals, which receive the water, and where it is foon abforbed by the fpongy earth. In the lower part of thefe fides he has likewife opened a number of cavities equally proper to furnifh alum.

The fame principle appears to have guided

guided the Abbé in his attempts to increase the quantity produced of sal-ammoniac, by making use of long and capacious tubes of earth, open at both extremities, and baked in the furnace. These receive, at their lower ends, the vapours abounding with this salt, which attaches itself to their inner sides, and forms there a crust, that in time increases to a considerable thickness. I have seen, with pleasure, at Naples, the effects of these two methods; and it is expected they will be still more productive, when some alterations suggested by persons well acquainted with this business have been made.

Formerly sulphur was extracted from the crater of this volcano; but the small quantity of it, and the low price of the commodity, have caused this labour to be abandoned.

Descending from Solfatara, a little above the level of the sea, and near to Pozzuolo, we meet with the ruins of a temple, supposed to have been dedicated to Serapis, and in

modern

modern times freed from a flimy eruption, under which it was buried. This edifice may at once gratify the admirer of the imitative arts, by its architecture, and the curiofity of the naturalift. Among the parts which ftill remain entire, are three beautiful columns of that fpecies of white Grecian marble, ufually called *cipollino*. They are erect, but, at the height of about nine feet from the ground, each column begins to appear worn; and this wearing extending round the column, forms a horizontal band, or fillet, which is rough and unequal, about two feet in breath, while the remainder of the column is fmooth and polifhed. This band is in every part bored by the marine animalcule called *Mytilus lithophagus* by Linnæus, and in fome of the perforations the fhells are ftill to be found, either entire or in fragments.

But befides this fpecies, which is well known to Conchiologifts, I have difcovered another, which I had before found, in a living ftate, in fome fubaqueous marbles in the

the lake of Venice, an accurate defcription of which I fhall referve for another work. Several of the fhells of this mytilus, which is fmaller than the other, are to be found in the perforations of this part of the column. In fact, on examining with attention, befides the holes made by the two fpecies of mytili already mentioned, I found many others, extremely fmall ones, which all who are acquainted with the different fpecies of marine animalcula, will know to be the work of other lithophagous worms. I muft likewife add that I have found among them fome ferpules, and particularly the *contortuplicata*, and the *triquetra* of Linnæus. Thefe are the marine animalcula which have eaten into the three columns near the middle of the fhaft, producing that circle of inequalities and roughnefs, except which there is no veftige of thefe animals.

On the plain of the Temple are found feveral other fragments of columns, fome of the fame *cipollino* marble with the former, and others of African marble; which fragments have likewife bands or fillets of inequalities and roughnefs fimilar to thofe before defcribed, above and below which the marble is perfectly fmooth, and ftill retains the polifh it originally received from the hand of the artift.

On the fame plain we fee, fcattered, feveral columns of granite, which appeared to me to be oriental; the component parts of which are black mica with large flakes, which is very abundant, a large proportion of felt-fpar, and quartz. But thefe columns have not been touched by the corroding worms; nor was it to be expected that they fhould, as it appears, from a variety of inftances, that they only attack calcareous ftone.

M. Ferber, in his letters before cited, mentions this appearance in the columns; but he only notices the *mytilus lithophagus*, which he calls the *pholas* or *dactylus*. But the cavities in which thefe pholades have lodged, being nine feet high above the prefent

fent level of the sea, he infers that the sea has sunk nine feet, supporting this inference by the observation " that the pholades always reside in rocks level with the surface of the water, and never are found near the bottom."

But this is an assumption contrary to fact, as I shall easily prove. The pholades in these columns, which, according to Linnæus and other systematic naturalists, belong to the genus of the mytili, I have very frequently found in the Gulf of Spezia at Genoa, and in its environs, within the port itself of that city, in several places in the sea of Istria, and other parts of the Adriatic, and likewise in the Mediterranean. But in all these places I have found them in subaqueous rocks, never, or scarcely ever, level with the surface of the water; and, frequently, I have procured them to be fished up from the bottom of the sea, at the depth of ten or twelve feet, by the means of long and stout forceps, which drew up large pieces of the rock, in which they were contained

tained in a living ſtate. I have, alſo, in my poſſeſſion, ſeveral of theſe pholades, or more properly ſpeaking mytili, infixed within the hard ſhells of very large oyſters fiſhed up in my preſence, from the depth of 142 feet. But in theſe columns we find not only the remains of mytili, but of ſerpules and of other very ſmall lithophagous worms which are found in the ſea at every depth. As, therefore, the ſuppoſition of Ferber, that the pholades or mytili always reſide at the ſurface of the water only, is contrary to fact, his deduction that the level of the ſea has ſunk nine feet, ſince the time of the corroding of theſe columns, muſt likewiſe evidently be erroneous. All that we can with certainty affirm is, that the circle, or fillet, which has been the habitation of theſe marine worms, has been covered by the ſea for a long ſeries of years; as may be inferred from the remains of theſe animals found in the cells they have ſunk, which ſhew that they had attained their perfect ſize, to complete which they require nearly half a century, as I could prove by inconteſtable facts,

did

did I not fear it would lead me too far from my fubject.

It may perhaps be objected that it muft appear extraordinary, that thefe columns, which are now in an erect pofition, fhould have been fo long wafhed by the fea-water in that circle only, while the part of the fhaft below it remained untouched. Yet might they not, before they were employed in the fabric of which they made a part, have been buried in the fea in fuch a manner that this circle alone, which is now rich with marine fpoils, might be acceffible to the water? But though this hypothefis fhould not appear fatisfactory, and I have no other to offer, I fhall content myfelf with ftating the facts of which I have knowledge, without feeling any great folicitude that I am not able to explain them.

CHAP.

CHAP. III.

THE GROTTO DEL CANE.

Errors of Ferber relative to this celebrated grotto—Experiments of the author and the Abbé Breiſlak, relative to the mortiferous vapour—Deſcription of the grotto—Conjecture that the vapour was anciently more extenſive—Its mean height—Its heat greater than that of the atmoſphere—Conſiſts of carbonic-acid gas, mixed with atmoſpheric air, and azotic gas—This carbonic acid, according to the Abbé Breiſlak, is the produce of the carbure of iron contained in volcanic ſubſtances, and combined with oxygene—The mephitic vapour exhibits no ſigns of magnetiſm or electricity—Phenomena which accompanied the burning of ſeveral ſubſtances placed within the vapour—Remarks of the author on the experiments of the Abbé Breiſlak, and his

con-

conjectures on the origin of this carbonic acid.

HAVING visited Solfatara, and the surrounding rocks, continuing my journey to the west, I soon arrived at the *Grotta del Cane*. There is no person conversant with literature who does not know that this name has been given to a small cavern between Naples and Pozzuolo, because if a dog be brought into it, and his nose held to the ground, he soon begins to breathe with difficulty, and loses all sense, and even life, if he be not speedily removed into the open and purer air. This grotto, though so celebrated both in ancient and modern times, in fact shares its fame with several other places which are endowed with the same deleterious quality; as it is only one of the almost innumerable pestiferous vapours in different parts of the world, especially in volcanic countries, which are quickly fatal both to brute animals and man, though they do not offer to the eye the slightest indication of their presence. They have been

mentioned

mentioned by a numerous lift of writers, whom I might cite, were I difpofed to make an unfeafonable parade of my reading. It is to be remarked that the greater part of thefe vapours are only temporary, whereas that of the Grotta del Cane is perpetual, and feems to have produced its deadly effects in the time of Pliny. A man ftanding erect fuffers nothing from it; as the mephitic vapour rifes only to a fmall height from the ground: I, therefore, entered it without danger; but, notwithftanding the moft attentive obfervation I could make, I could not perceive the fmalleft vifible exhalation.

It therefore appeared to me that M. Ferber muft have been miftaken, when he fays, " the killing damps rife from the ground, " about a palm above the floor, move along " it as a white fmoke, and fpread through " the door in the open air *," But, as it has already been obferved that the fmoke of

---

* Ferber's Travels through Italy, p. 146, of the Englifh tranflation.

a torch

a torch extinguished in the vapour sinks downwards, assumes a whitish colour, and goes out at the bottom of the door; it appears probable that this occasioned his mistake, especially as he mentions the experiment of the extinguished torch in the same place.

As little can I agree with him that the mischievous effects of this vapour are the consequence of the air being deprived of its elasticity *; since it has been demonstrated that they are to be attributed to the carbonic-acid gas; as was first proved by his learned countryman, M. Adolphus Murray. As we know, likewise, that, a candle being extinguished in this gas, the fumes which proceed from it mix more readily with the gas than with the atmospheric air; we perceive why the smoke of a torch that ceases to burn in the Grotta del Cane, sinks where the pestiferous vapour is strongest, and, passing along the ground, goes out at the lower part of the door.

* Ferber's Travels.

The person who is the keeper, or guide, at the grotto, and who shews to strangers the experiment of the dog for a gratuity, when the animal is panting, and half dead, takes him into the open air, and afterwards throws him into the neighbouring lake of Agnano; insinuating that this short immersion into the water is necessary completely to restore him. M. Ferber relates this fact, and shews that he believed all that was told him concerning it. The truth however is, that the plunging the dog into the lake is a mere trick, to render the experiment more specious, and obtain money from the credulous, as the atmospheric air alone is sufficient to restore the animal to life.

The experiments made by M. Murray, to ascertain the nature of this mephitic vapour, have discovered to us what was before unknown, and we owe to him every grateful acknowledgment. They have not, however, explained every thing we could wish to learn relative to this cavern. Whoever is versed in the knowledge of nature, and acquainted, in any degree, with the difficult art of making experiments, muſt be convinced what a number of theſe might be made in it, which would greatly tend to throw new light on phyſiology and phyſics. I conceived a ſtrong deſire to attempt ſeveral, and communicated my intention to the Abbé Breiſlak, who accompanied me to the Grotta del Cane. We agreed to divide them between us, that I ſhould apply myſelf to the phyſiological, or thoſe which had for their object living beings, and he beſtow his attention on the phyſical. As I was on the point of ſetting out for Sicily, I reſolved to carry this plan into execution on my return to Naples. But Mount Etna and the Lipari iſles detained me a long time; and when I returned I had ſcarcely time to viſit Veſuvius, being obliged to repair almoſt immediately to Padua, to begin my public lectures in Natural Hiſtory. My friend, the Abbé, however, who reſides conſtantly near Solfatara, in conſequence of his ſuperintendance of the works there, proceeded, after my departure, to fulfil the taſk I had aſſigned him, and communicated to me the reſult of

his

his experiments in a letter, which, with his confent, I here publifh, as I am convinced that it will be highly gratifying to my readers.

Naples, November 20, 1790.

RESPECTABLE FRIEND,

WHEN you vifited this city, two years ago, to make obfervations on the Phlegrean Fields, you did me the honour to propofe to me to affift you in making a regular feries of experiments on the celebrated mephitic vapour of the Grotta del Cane. You may remember that we agreed to divide between us the objects to be examined. You propofed to inquire in what manner the exhalation acts on the animal œconomy, fo as firft to fufpend its functions, and at laft totally deftroy them, unlefs the means of reftoration are fpeedily applied. This problem, though confidered by many, has never been inveftigated with that precifion and accuracy which it deferves, nor have experiments been fufficiently multiplied and diverfified to eftablifh a general law. From you I expected that it would

would have received new light, accustomed as you are to develop the most complicated arcana of nature. In the experiments to be made, you reserved to yourself the physiological, leaving to me the physico-chemical. Your journey into Sicily, and your hasty return to Padua, to exercise the duties of your professorship, rendered it impossible at that time for you to execute your part of the plan. I have not dared to treat a subject reserved for you, but I hope that some other, to me fortunate, combination of circumstances may once more bring you back to Naples, and afford you an opportunity to prosecute these inquiries, together with others analogous to them. In the mean time, in some excursions which I have made to the lake Agnano, I have examined, with the utmost attention, this little grotto; and have made several experiments, by the detail of which I doubt not but you will be gratified. The subject, it is true, has been repeatedly examined by many naturalists, both natives of Italy and foreigners; but their success has not

not been sufficient to preclude every new experiment.

The mephitic vapour, as you well know, occupies the floor of a small grotto near the lake Agnano, a place highly interesting to naturalists from the phenomena its environs present, and the hills within which it is included. This grotto is situated on the south-east side of the lake, at a little distance from it. Its length is about twelve feet, and its breadth from four to five. It appears to have been originally a small excavation, made for the purpose of obtaining puzzolana. In the sides of the grotto, among the earthy volcanic matters, are found pieces of lava, of the same kind with those we meet with scattered near the lake. I examined some of them, and found them a compact lava, of a deep grey colour, interspersed with small hexaedrous prisms of mica. They are of an earthy grain, a micaceous consistence, and have a sensible effect on the magnet. Particles of feltspar are rarely found in them,

and

and we meet with no specimens which contain shoerls. I am persuaded that were new excavations made in the vicinity of the grotto, at a level with its floor, or a little lower, the same mephitic vapour would be found, and it would certainly be curious to ascertain the limits of its extent. It would likewise be extremely advantageous for physical observations, were the grotto somewhat enlarged, and its floor reduced to a level horizontal plain, by lowering it two or three feet, and surrounding it by a low wall, with steps at the entrance. In its present state, it is extremely inconvenient for experiments, and the inclination of the ground towards the door causes a great part of the vapour, from the effect of its specific gravity, to make its way out close to the ground. When I consider the narrow limits of this place, and the small quantity of the vapour which has rendered it so celebrated, I have no doubt but it must have undergone considerable changes; for it does not appear probable to me that Pliny meant only the present confined vapour, when (lib. ii. cap. 93),

enumerating many places from which a deadly air exhaled, he mentions the territory of Pozzuolo. The internal fermentations by which it is caused are certainly much diminished in the vicinity of the lake Agnano. The water near its banks is no longer seen to bubble up, from the disengagement of a gas, as we learn that it formerly did, from accounts of no very great antiquity. I have attentively examined the borders of the lake, when its waters were at the highest, and after heavy rains, but I never could discover a single bubble of air. A number of aquatic insects, which sport on the surface, may, at first view, occasion some deception; but a little observation will detect the error. If we do not suppose those authors who have described the ebullition of the water near the banks of the lake Agnano to have been deceived, we must at least confess that this phenomenon has now ceased. The quantity of the hepatic vapours, which rise in the contiguous stoves, called the stoves of St. Germano, must likewise be greatly diminished from what it anciently was: for, adjoining to the present stoves, we still find
the

the remains of a spacious ancient fabric, with tubes of terra cotta inserted in the walls, which, by their direction, shew for what purpose they were intended. It appears certain that this was a building in which, by the means of pipes properly disposed, the vapours of the place were introduced into different rooms, for the use of patients, who were accommodated there in a much better manner than they are in the modern stoves of St. Germano, which wretched places nothing could induce them to endure but the hope of being restored to health. To these ruins, however, the vapours no longer extend; so that, if this edifice still remained, it could not be employed for the purpose for which it was intended. The veins of pyrites which have produced the more ancient conflagrations of the Phlegrean fields, between Naples and Cuma, and which, in some places, are entirely consumed, approach their total extinction. But let us proceed to the experiments made, and frequently repeated, within the grotto.

I. The firſt had for its object to determine the height of the mephitis, at the centre of the grotto, that is, at the interſection of the line of its greateſt length with that of its greateſt breadth. This height varies according to the different diſpoſitions and temperatures of the atmoſphere, the diverſity of winds, and the accidental variations that take place in the internal fermentations by which the vapour is produced; it may, however, be eſtimated, at a mean, at eight Paris inches.

II. The entrance into the mephitis is accompanied with a ſlight ſenſation of heat, in the feet and lower part of the legs. When, in the year 1786, I viſited the larger mephitic vapours of Latera, in the duchy of Caſtro, I likewiſe obſerved that they produced the ſenſation of heat in the part of the body which was encompaſſed by the mephitic atmoſphere. Yet on taking out of the vapour ſeveral ſubſtances which had remained in it a long time, as ſtones, leaves, carcaſes of animals, &c. I found that theſe were of the ſame temperature with the atmoſpheric mofpheric air; but as I had broken my thermometer on the road, and was unable to procure another in any of the places through which I paffed, I could not afcertain the temperature of the mephitis. I felt in my body a flight degree of heat, which I could not perceive in the fubftances I took out of the mephitic vapour; and endeavouring to compare one thing with another, I concluded that the temperature of the mephitis was the fame with that of the atmofpheric air, which I attempted to explain to myfelf on the principles laid down by Dr. Crawford. But a number of other experiments, made in the Grotta del Cane, have convinced me that this exhalation has a diftinct degree of heat, different from that of the atmofphere. In thefe experiments, which I repeated many times, the thermometer, fufpended at the aperture of the grotto, three feet above the furface of the mephitis, ftood at between 13 and 14 of Reaumur's fcale (62 and 64 of Fahrenheit's); and, placing the ball on the ground, fo that it was immerfed in the mephitic vapour, the mercury arofe to between

21 and 22 of Reaumur (80 and 82 of Fahrenheit.) Nor ought it to excite furprife, that the fubftances taken out of the mephitis did not exhibit this diverfity of temperature, both becaufe the difference is fmall, and on account of the quantity of humidity with which they are always loaded, and which produces on their furface a continual evaporation. I frequently repeated this experiment, making ufe of different thermometers, becaufe I knew that the celebrated M. Adolphus Murray, when he made his experiments in the Grotta del Cane, had not obferved the vapour to produce any effect on the mercury in the thermometer.

III. I repeated, for my own fatisfaction, the ufual experiments, made by many naturalifts, with the tincture of turnfole, limewater, the cryftallizations of alkalis, the abforption of water, and the acidulous tafte communicated to it, which prove beyond all doubt the exiftence of fixed air, or carbonic acid, in the exhalation of which we treat. But is it compofed of fixed air alone? This
I wifhed

I wished to ascertain. When exposed in a eudiometer to nitrous gas, an absorption took place, to about the $\frac{10}{100}$ of the quantity. In a phial filled with this air, and continued with the mouth immersed in water for fifteen days, the water slowly rose until it occupied $\frac{40}{100}$: it may, therefore, be concluded that the relative quantities of the different gases which compose the mephitic air of the Grotta del Cane are as follows: $\frac{10}{100}$ of vital air, or oxygenous gas, $\frac{40}{100}$ of fixed air, or carbonic acid, and $\frac{50}{100}$ of phlogisticated air, or azotic gas; or perhaps it is a mixture of carbonic acid and atmospheric air, with a small quantity of azotic gas, more than is contained in the atmospheric air.

The vicinity of the grotto to the stoves of Agnano, the warm vapours of which contain a considerable quantity of hydrogenous sulphurated gas, induced me to suspect that some portion of the latter might be found mixed with the gas of the mephitis; but I was not able to discover in it the smallest quantity. I made use of the sugar of lead,

lead, or acetite of lead, which, as you well know, is extremely fenfible to the flighteft impreffion of hepatic gas, leaving it immerfed in the mephitis for the fpace of half an hour.

It is certainly a curious problem to inveftigate the origin of this fixed air. You are acquainted with the different opinions of naturalifts, fome of whom confider it as atmofpheric air, changed into fixed by the action of the electric matter of the lava; while others fuppofe it produced by a flow and fucceffive decompofition of the calcareous earth, effected, either by a fubterraneous fire, or by an acid. But the fact is, that, in the Grotta del Cane, there is not a fingle vein of lava, and that the atmofphere of that vicinity exhibits no particular figns of electricity. The hypothefis founded on the decompofition of the calcareous earth, is, likewife, fubject to great difficulties. Our excellent common friend, the Commendatory de Dolomieu, in his valuable notes to the differtations of Bergman on the products of volcanos, is of opinion that the fixed air of volcanic

canic places is produced by the re-action of the fulphur on the calcareous earth, with which it forms a liver of earthy fulphur. I am rather inclined to believe that the fixed air of volcanized countries is not developed ready formed from any fubftance, but is the produce of the plumbago contained in the iron, with which all volcanic fubftances abound, combined with the bafe of vital air afforded by the internal decompofitions of the pyrites. I am not induced to embrace this fyftem by its novelty. The experiments of Meffieurs Lavoifier, Berthollet, Mongez, Landriani, and many other excellent chemifts, compared with local obfervations, have proved, beyond a doubt, the exiftence of plumbago in iron. It is certain that all volcanic fubftances abound in iron, and the hepatic vapours which rife in the ftoves of St. Germano, in the vicinity of the Grotta del Cane, prove the internal decompofition of the pyrites, which ftill takes place here: a decompofition, which, by giving birth to the mephitic acid, furnifhes likewife the bafe of vital air.

IV.

IV. Among the notices which the celebrated Bergman wished to receive, relative to the Grotta del Cane, he defired a detail of the phenomena of magnetifm and electricity. With refpect to the former, I have obferved no new appearance. The magnetic needle, placed on the ground, and confequently immerfed in the mephitis, refted in the direction of its meridian; and, at the approach of a magnetized bar, exhibited the ufual effects of attraction and repulfion, according as either pole was prefented. With regard to the latter article, it is not poffible to make electrical experiments, within the mephitis; not becaufe that kind of air is a conductor of the electric fluid, as M. Murray imagined, but becaufe the humidity that conftantly accompanies it, difperfes the electric matter, which not being collected in a conductor, cannot be rendered fenfible. I, feveral times, attempted to fire inflammable gas, in the mephitic vapour, with electric fparks, by means of the conductor of the electrophorus; but, notwithftanding my utmoft endeavours to animate the electricity,

I never

I never could obtain a single spark; as the isolator became a conductor, the moment it entered into the mephitis, on account of the humidity which adhered to its surface.

V. One of the principal objects of the researches of academies and naturalists, at present, is the theory of the combustion of bodies. My first experiment was directed to ascertain whether those spontaneous inflammations which result from the mixture of concentrated acids with essential oils could be obtained. I placed on the ground, in the grotto, a small vessel, in such a situation that the mephitis rose six inches above the edges of the vessel. I made use of oil of turpentine, and the vitriolic and nitrous acids, and the same inflammation followed, accompanied with a lively flame, as would have taken place in the open atmospheric air. The dense smoke, which always accompanies these inflammations, attracted by the humidity of the mephitis, presented its undulations to the eye, and formed a very pleasing object. As I had put a considerable quantity of acid

in

in the veffel, I repeatedly poured in a little of the oil, and the flame appeared in the mouth of the veffel fifteen times fucceffively. The oxygenous principle, contained in the acids, and with which the nitrous acid principally abounds, undoubtedly contributed to the production and duration of this flame, though enveloped in an atmofphere inimical to inflammation.

In the diftrict of Latera, which I have mentioned above, I obferved that, in a mephitis of hydrogenous fulphurated gas, or hepatic gas, a flow combuftion of phofphorus took place, with the fame refplendence as in the atmofpheric air. As I had not with me a fufficient quantity of phofphorus, I could not proceed farther with this experiment, nor vary it as might have been neceffary. In the mephitis of Agnano, the firft experiment I made was with common phofphoric matches, of which I broke five, holding them clofe to the ground, and, confequently, immerfed in the mephitis. They all produced a fhort and tranfient flame,

flame, which became extinguished the moment it was communicated to the wick of a candle. The second experiment I made was the following. I placed on the ground, in the grotto, a long table, in such a manner that one end of it was without the mephitis, while the other, and four fifths of its whole length, were immersed in it. Along this table, I laid a train of gunpowder, beginning from the end without the mephitis; and, at the other, which was immersed within it, the depth of seven inches, I placed, adjoining to the gunpowder, a cylinder of phosphorus, eight lines in length. The gunpowder without the mephitis being fired, the combustion was soon communicated to the other extremity of the train, and to the phosphorus, which took fire with decrepitation, burnt rapidly, with a bright flame, slightly coloured with yellow and green, and left on the wood a black mark, as of charcoal. The combustion lasted nearly two minutes, till the whole phosphoric matter was consumed.

I then

I then proceeded to another experiment. I placed some gunpowder on the ground in the grotto; and having lighted a cylinder of phosphorus without the mephitis, I immerged it within it, while burning, carried it the distance of ten feet, and threw it on the gunpowder, which immediately took fire. No alteration was perceptible in the flame, or manner of burning, of the lighted phosphorus, either at the moment of its entrance into the mephitis, or during its continuance in it.

I afterwards lighted another cylinder of phosphorus, and conveyed it immediately into the mephitis, supporting it with a small piece of wood: and this, likewise, burnt briskly, until it was entirely consumed.

It may, perhaps, be suspected that, in the experiments with gunpowder, the oxygenous gas contained in the nitre co-operated to the combustion of the phosphorus; but it is certain that, independent of the nitre, this curious substance, though it burnt in

mephitic

mephitic air, prefented the fame appearances as in the atmofpheric air. I am aware that, among the experiments of M. Lavoifier, there is one on the combuftion of phofphorus produced by means of a burning mirror, under a glafs bell, the mouth of which was immerfed in mercury. That excellent naturalift obferved that the phofphorus began to burn, but that, in a few moments, the air of the receiver being no longer proper to nourifh the combuftion, it became extinguifhed. Is it not probable that the extinction of the phofphorus did not proceed from the infection of the air, but that the vapours of the phofphoric matter remaining confined in the receiver, and condenfing around the phofphorus, fuffocated its flame ? The mephitic gas of the Grotta del Cane is certainly unfit for the refpiration of animals, and the inflammation of common combuftible fubftances; but phofphorus, neverthelefs, burns in it, and emits, as ufual, luminous fparks.

I must not conclude without noticing the production of the phosphoric acid from the slow combustion of phosphorus in the mephitis. Perhaps this may present particular modifications, dependent on the carbonic acid, to which it must necessarily unite itself in this situation. But I have not yet been able to prosecute this experiment, the temperature of the place not being such as is requisite to make use of the apparatus suited to the method of M. Sage. I shall therefore defer the investigation of this subject until the winter, when I purpose to resume it, if I can procure free access to the grotto, for some little time, by satisfying the avidity of its rapacious guardian.

I remain,

With sentiments of the utmost

Friendship and esteem,

Your devoted servant and friend,

SCIPIO BREISLAK.

The observations and experiments communicated in the above letter, undoubtedly, enlarge very considerably the sphere of our knowledge, relative to this mephitic place; and I sincerely congratulate the author on the success of his researches. But the same sincerity induces me to mention an observation which occurred to me while reading his letter, and which, I am convinced, his friendship will permit me to make public. The method he used to obtain the mortiferous gas on which he made the experiments here related, was, I doubt not, the same with that employed to ascertain the salubrity of the atmospheric air; that is, by taking a phial filled with water, inverting, and plunging it into the mephitis, then letting the water gradually out, and carefully closing the phial. Had any other method been used, I doubt not but it would have been mentioned. But by this the mephitis could not be obtained pure, such as it immediately issues from the floor of the grotto, but must be more or less mixed with atmospheric air. For the carbonic acid gas being heavier than the atmospheric air, it must consequently form a stratum in the lower parts of the grotto, where it will, in general, remain, though there will be some mixture of the two fluids; especially when the door is opened, and the internal ambient air put in motion. Hence the mixture of the three gases, the carbonic acid, the azotic, and the oxygenous, obtained by the Abbé Breislak. I had, however, suggested to him, that the best method to obtain this emanation pure would be to dig a small trench in the ground of the grotto, and to fill it with water; when a number of bubbles would, no doubt, rise from the bottom to the surface, which would probably only consist of the carbonic acid gas suspended in the body of the water. The contents of these bubbles might be collected by methods well known, and we should thus procure the genuine mephitis, without any mixture of atmospheric air. For greater accuracy in the experiment, mercury might be placed under the water; as it seems probable that the tufaceous soil would be sufficiently dense to retain it.

We have seen the opinion of this learned naturalist,

naturalist, relative to the origin of the carbonic acid in this grotto. It is evident that, in this, as in many other questions of a similar kind, we can only amuse ourselves with conjecture, and perhaps we may never be able to proceed farther than conjecture, relative to an operation which nature has veiled in profound obscurity, and withdrawn from the observation of our senses. But since certainty is not attainable, I must ingenuously declare, that among the different hypotheses that have been framed to account for this abstruse phenomenon, I prefer that which supposes that the mephitis of the Grotta del Cane is separated, by the means of fire, from carbonates of lime (or calcareous earths), and that, passing through different volcanic substances, it has penetrated to that place. It is highly probable that the volcanos of the Neapolitan territory, and also those of the ecclesiastical state, are superincumbent on strata of such carbonates, continued and connected with those of the Apennines. In my way from Lombardy to Naples, when I arrived in the neighbourhood of Loretto, the road began to lead between mountains, which continued to Fuligno, a diftance of nearly feventy miles. Thefe mountains, almoft all with horizontal ftrata, are compofed of thefe carbonates. The road from Fuligno to Spoleto and Terni prefents a chain of mountains of the fame kind, and nearly with the fame ftratifications. Thefe mountains extended to within a little diftance of Civita Caftellana, where I found fufficient teftimonies of extinct volcanos, in the puzzolana and lavas, which I met with at every ftep. Some of thefe lavas are of a bafe of fhoerl in the mafs, and others of a horn-ftone bafe: they all refemble the Vefuvian with refpect to the white garnets they contain. The volcanic bodies, and various kinds of tufa and puzzolana, continued to prefent themfelves quite to the gates of Rome. From this city, continuing my journey to Naples, by the way of Veletri, I continually met with volcanized matters; but, at Terracina, the mountains next the fea again appeared to be formed of calcareous earth, as did thofe of Seffa.

But,

But, whatever may be the character of the more elevated parts, the bottoms, through which the high road passes, consist of tufa, which exhibits the true signs of volcanisation not only in the pieces of lava, and the great number of pumices it contains, but from being in a great degree a mixture of small fragments of lava and scoria.

It is to be remarked, and it is worthy of attentive consideration, that when we leave the road, and ascend the steep eminences on its sides, we frequently find beneath the tufa, calcareous stone, especially in places where the former has been corroded by rain water. The remainder of the Apennines from Sessa to Naples are formed of the same calcareous stone; though, in lower situations, the volcanic tufa is scarcely ever interrupted.

In Chap. VI. I shall speak of a volcano which I observed near Caserta, a small city about sixteen miles from Naples. I shall then shew that the volcanic matters are there

there every where furrounded by calcareous ftone.

The Foffa Grande, which defcends laterally from Mount Vefuvius, and which I have mentioned in Chap. I. is bordered on the fides by two high rocks. That which is on the left, the fide towards Naples, owes its origin to an aggregate of lava; while that on the right is compofed of pumice-ftone and tufa; which not being firmly connected frequently fall by their own weight, efpecially when loofened by rains, and, in their fall, bring down with them various fubftances, of which fome are calcareous fpars, mixed with pieces of the common calcareous earth, which, as I have already mentioned, I met with in my journey to Naples. Thefe fubftances feldom exhibit any traces of injury by the fire: their angles, likewife, are not blunt or ragged, but fharp. It is, however, indubitable that they are pieces rent from great maffes of calcareous ftone, before the vehemence of the

fire

fire had time to change them. These observations I made on my return from Vesuvius to Naples.

The author of the *Campi Phlegræi*, speaking incidentally of the Fossa Grande, gives the figure of a piece of calcareous breccia found there; and observes that similar pieces are frequently found in the excavations made by the rains in the sides of Vesuvius and Monte Somma. The *Lithologia Gioeniana*, which treats on the productions of this volcano, mentions similar calcareous stones to have been thrown up from its mouths in former times.

The island of Capri, near Naples, it is to be observed, is likewise composed of calcareous earth.

From all these observations, it appears to admit of no doubt that the Neapolitan territory, which we see volcanized, rests on calcareous strata. This was likewise the opinion of Ferber and Sir William Hamilton.

If,

If, then, we suppose the subterraneous fire to act gradually on the calcareous stone, compelling it to divest itself by degrees of its acid, while it becomes covered with earthy aggregations easily permeable to this acid, now become gaseous, the gas will issue above it, and form a current mingling with the atmospheric air. This, probably, will explain the nature of the emanation in the Grotta del Cane. The Abbé Brieslak has shewn that the heat of this emanation is greater than that of the atmosphere; which affords us reason to suppose that a remainder of volcanic fire exists under the grotto. The great humidity of the vapour is, likewise, extremely favourable to this hypothesis, since we know that calcareous stone, by the action of fire, is not only deprived of its acid, but of the water which it contained. It may be objected that, on this supposition, the mephitis must diminish; but it should be considered that its extent is very confined, while the quantity of the subjacent calcareous matter is immense; and it is likewise

well

well known what a prodigious quantity of this acid is combined with such stones.

This hypothesis will likewise explain the temporary mephites, which arise only in consequence of particular eruptions, as frequently happens in the environs of Vesuvius. The deleterious exhalations will continue till the subterraneous fires have decomposed the calcareous stones; but they cease when the conflagrations are extinguished.

CHAP. IV.

LAKES OF AGNANO AND AVERNO—MONTE NUOVO—PROMONTORY AND CAVERN OF MISENO—ROCK OF BURNT STONES—PROCIDA.

The lake of Agnano once a spacious volcanic crater—Tenches and frogs found in this lake—The absurd report that monstrous animals are produced there, detected by Vallisneri—The lake of Averno presents the mouth of another ancient volcano—It is false that birds cannot approach this lake—No deleterious exhalation emitted by it—Volcanic substances of Monte Nuovo—Lavas found there of the nature of pumice and smalt—Soda grows in a little cavern of its crater—Peculiarity of amphibious animals observed here—The cavern of Miseno abounds in sulphate of alumine (alum) and pumice—Well of water full

full of gaseous bubbles. Volcanic crater still discernible on the promontory of Miseno —Pumices found there, containing feltspars. Lava, pumices, and enamels of the same nature, found on the Rock of Burnt Stones, and at Procida—Great friability of this enamel, not common to volcanic enamels, and its probable cause.

THOUGH the Phlegrean fields are numerous, I in this work propose to describe or at least to give a sketch of them all; since, though they are all volcanic, the objects they present are few, and little different from each other.

I believe no one doubts that the cavity filled with water, and usually denominated the lake of Agnano, has been the mouth of a volcano. It certainly has internally the resemblance of one, since it is shaped like an inverted funnel, the usual figure of volcanic craters. It must have been a very large one, since it is nearly two miles in circuit. Numerous flocks of ducks swim on its surface,

and

and its waters contain great quantities of tenches and frogs, which were once celebrated for a pretended monstrous formation: until the cause of this absurd error was detected by Vallisneri. It may not, perhaps, be uninstructive, should I, by way of an amusing digression, relate the story of this pleasant mistake to the reader.

It is well known that frogs, before they arrive at the perfect form of their species, have that of a kind of worms, usually called tadpoles; the bodies of which are of an orbicular shape, and have tails. We know likewise that these tadpoles become frogs by degrees, the hinder legs being first produced, and afterwards the fore-legs, while they retain the tail for a considerable time. This gives them a strange appearance, as the tail appears like the lower half of a fish, while the round body and legs resemble the frog. Hence persons unacquainted with the productions of nature have supposed them to be monstrous animals, half fish and half frogs. A credulous Neapolitan brought one of these

monsters,

monsters which he said was a native of the lake Agnano, to Vallisneri, at Milan, that he might view it and admire. It did not, however, require the knowledge of so great a naturalist immediately to perceive the absurd error. The tadpole, which to him was an object of laughter, not of admiration, was of an extraordinary size, whence he concluded that the frogs of the lake Agnano were extremely large. They are not, however, larger than the common size, nor did I find the tadpoles bigger, though, as it was the end of July, they had arrived at their full growth, and many, having cast their tails, had become perfect frogs. That which was shewn to Vallisneri was, possibly, brought from some other country, perhaps America; where the frogs grow to an extremely large size.

The sides and bottom of this lake are of tufa, intersperfed, in some places, with fragments of lava and pumice-stone; though we do not find, at least so far as the eye can reach, any veins or strata of lava: whence I infer the eruption to have been
entirely,

entirely, or in a great degree, thick and flimy.

The fame ideas which naturally occur to the obferver at fight of the lake Agnano, will be fuggefted, likewife, by that of Averno, as there can be no doubt but this likewife was the crater of an ancient volcano. The Greeks called it *Aornus;* becaufe no birds were found near it, probably on account of fome peftilential vapour which then exhaled, and deprived them of life. The author of the *Campi Phlegræi* afferts that it is very rarely that any water-fowl are to be feen on this lake, and that when they come they remain there but a very fhort time. The truth, however, is, that, whenever I was there, I faw great numbers of teal fwimming on the furface; and the peafants affured me that the lake abounded with water-fowl in the winter. Nor do I know any caufe which can, at prefent, drive them from a place where they may find plenty of food; as neither the environs, nor the lake itfelf, afford any indication of noxious exhalations.

Thefe

These two places lie to the west of Naples, near Pozzuolo, in the vicinity of which is Monte Nuovo, so called because it was produced by subterranean fires in 1538. It is not very high, and, seen from the port of Pozzuolo, appears to be an obtuse cone; but, on reaching the top, we discover that this cone is only the exterior part of a crater, the upper edges of which form a circle of about one hundred and fifty feet in diameter.

Like other volcanic craters, the internal sides of this grow narrow towards the bottom, and both that which I call the bottom, and the external part of Monte Nuovo, consist of a friable tufa, in many places, covered with plants. The sea bathes the sides of this volcano, which, if they are dug into a little, as well within the water as without, are found very warm. The same warmth is likewise perceived at the bottom of the crater. From such excavations, likewise, arise thin warm vapours. In fact, in the internal parts of Monte Nuovo we find all the laſt remains of volcanic conflagration.

In the external ſides of the mountain many pieces of lava are found, which deſerve notice from their ſingular quality. They are a ſubſtance of a middle character between lava and pumice-ſtone, on which account I ſhall call them pumice-lavas. They have the lightneſs and friability of a compact pumice-ſtone. When broken by the teeth, by which a good judgment may be formed of ſome ſtones, they appear real pumice-ſtone. They are dry and rough to the touch, as is uſual with ſuch kinds of volcanic productions. Their ſtructure is not fibrous, contrary to what we obſerve in common pumice-ſtone, but granulous, and very ſimilar to that of various kinds of lava, as is likewiſe the internal appearance. This production is of importance, as preſenting a middle ſubſtance between lava and pumice-ſtone. The baſe of theſe ſtones is a horn-ſtone, mixed with a few feltſpar ſcales:

they scarcely adhere to the tongue, and emit a slight argillaceous odour. In the furnace they produce a compact enamel, of a dark grey colour, transparent at the angles, and which gives a few sparks with steel.

Towards the internal bottom of the crater we find, projecting from the tufa, the same kind of lava, penetrated with feltspars, but more compact and heavy, and interspersed with beautiful and shining veins of black enamel of various thickness. I am in doubt whether this species of vitrification was the consequence of a greater degree of heat to which the lava had been there exposed, or whether, from the difference of its quality, in those places, it had undergone a more perfect fusion, and become enamel, while in others it had remained in the state of lava.

On the side of this bottom we find, within the tufa, a small cavity, I know not whether formed by nature or art, that abounds with saline

saline efflorescences, which I at firſt imagined to be muriate of ammoniac (ſal ammoniac), or ſulphate of alumine (alùm); but their urinous acrid taſte, the green colour which they gave to ſyrup of violets, and other qualities that are proper to ſoda, and which I omit for the ſake of brevity, leave no doubt that they are formed from that ſalt. Beſides theſe efflorescences, the ſmall hollows, corners, and bottom, of this cavity are more or leſs covered with the duſt of this ſoda.

I cannot take leave of this volcano without mentioning an obſervation, which has ſome analogy to what has been before noticed of lake Agnano, as it relates to the ſame ſpecies of animals. On the tufaceous ſides of the crater, both internal and external, as often as I approached them, I ſaw a great number of frogs leaping about. They were nearly half an inch long, and a quarter in breadth. They had the complete form of the frog, were of a dark-yellow colour, and their fore-feet were divided into four toes, and

and their hinder into five, though they have not the shape of the hand, which constitutes an essential difference between these frogs and the others of these countries. But how are these amphibious animals produced? Among all the different species of European frogs (and, under this genus, I, with Linnæus, likewise include toads) I know none which do not begin their existence in water, and continue to live in it some time, until they throw off the mask of the tadpole, and assume the shape of frogs. But Monte Nuovo is not only entirely without moisture, but, as I learned from the peasants who reside in the neighbourhood, even when heavy rains fall, the bottom of the crater (which is the only place where rain-water can be collected and retained) imbibes all the water immediately; as, in fact, it must, since it consists of a light spongy tufa full of cracks and fissures.

The only water near, is that of the lake Agnano, about half a mile distant; from which these animals might be supposed to have derived their origin, were it not that the

frogs

frogs of that lake are of a totally different species. I muft therefore confefs, that the prefence of thefe creatures here was to me an enigma, which, perhaps, I might have been able to have folved, not without fome advantage to natural knowledge, had I been able to have made a longer ftay in this volcanic country.

Before we reach the promontory of Mifeno we arrive at the harbour, which is a very fecure bafon, as it is furrounded on every fide by eminences. This was the port for the Roman fleet in the Mediterranean. The eminences are of tufa; and, on one fide, a little above the level of the fea, we find a fpacious cavity, the work of art, called the Cavern of Mifeno, in which the muriate of alumine continually efflorefces. This falt is either unknown to or neglected by the inhabitants; though it might be extracted with great advantage, efpecially were the cavern enlarged (which it might eafily be, as the tufa is extremely foft), fince the faline efflorefcences would certainly increafe

in

in proportion to the enlargement of the superficies.

At the bottom of the cavern there is a well of water bubbling up, with sometimes more, sometimes fewer, gaseous bubbles, which rise from the bottom. The water is nearly of the same temperature with the atmosphere, and the gas, from the scent, appears to be sulphurated hydrogenous; but I had not convenient opportunity exactly to ascertain its quality. The sides and roof of the cavern are scattered over with common pumices, containing various feltspars, some calcined, and consequently deprived of their native lustre, without, however, having lost their natural crystallization, which is rhomboidal.

Beyond the port of Miseno is the promontory of the same name, which forms a tufaceous mountain of no despicable height; from the top of which some admirable prospects present themselves. This, likewise, certainly owes its origin to a volcano, as its crater

crater is still very discernible, though in a great measure destroyed, on the south side, by the waves of the sea.

Having proceeded to some distance from this promontory, I met with several lavas immersed in the tufa, both of the compact and porous species, but common to other volcanos, and all detached. Mixed with these were various pieces of pumice, in like manner detached, in which feltspars were, I will not say, scattered, but thickly sown. In a square inch of this pumice I counted fourteen on the exterior surface, and forty-seven within. They are crystallized with various faces, are somewhat less hard than quartz, and have that changeable brilliancy which is inseparable from feltspars. The fire does not appear to have been able to injure them, though it has changed their base into pumice, which is in fact a real vitrification.

In front of Procida, and at a little distance from it, a small low rock projects into the sea, formerly only known to fishermen, and called

called the *Rock of Burnt Stones*, becaufe it is, in fact, a mixture of pumices, enamels, and lavas. The firſt naturaliſt who noticed it was the Abbé Brieſlak, who conducted me to it with a particular kind of pleaſure, as a place appertaining to himſelf. A ſtay of two hours, which I made on it, was well rewarded by the objects it preſented. Its elevation above the ſurface of the water is only a few feet, and conſequently, in tempeſtuous weather, it muſt be covered by the waves. On making the circuit of it in a boat, and examining it, we find that only the projecting points riſe above the water, and that the body of the rock is below the ſurface. Hence it appears probable, that it was once much larger, but has been in a great degree deſtroyed by the violence of the waves.

The ſtones of which this rock is compoſed are principally of two qualities. The firſt, a lava of a horn-ſtone baſe, light, of a dark grey colour, an earthy grain, unequal, and which gives ſcarcely any ſparks with ſteel.

steel. The second is a lava, with a base of shoerl in the mass, which has undergone various changes and modifications, according to the different heats to which it has been exposed. In many fragments, therefore, we only find it a simple lava, while, in others, it has become pumice, and in others enamel. Some pieces attract our observation, by being partly converted into pumice, and partly into enamel. In one part they appear of a whitish colour, fibrous, light, and extremely friable; but, as their levity and friability diminish, they become more compact, and the fibres less discernible; the colour grows darker, and a glassy lustre begins to appear. A little farther, their fibrous quality is entirely lost; their compactness, weight, hardness, and lustre increase, and the unequivocal characters of a perfect enamel are seen. This latter is black, gives sparks with steel, and in its appearance resembles the asphaltum. Its black colour is interrupted by feltspars, which are likewise common to the first lava with the horn-stone base. They are extremely brilliant,

ant, somewhat fibrous, crystallized in hexaedrous prisms, and several of them five lines in length.

It frequently happens, that the volcanic productions which exist in one place are found likewise in another: that is, that, in different situations, the earthy matters and the activity of the fire have been the same; a concurrence which may easily take place in various parts of the globe; and which is exemplified in the similarity of a corner of the island of Procida to the Rock of Burnt Stones. The island is situated to the west of the rock, and is about six leagues in circuit. The shore, being an accumulated mass of tufa, abounds with shrubs and plants. This tufa, on the side next Ischia, having been much corroded by the sea, affords a distinct view of its structure, which is in strata; whence we may infer that it has been the production of successive fluid depositions. To the north-west of the island is a rock, on which we find pumices, pumiceous lavas, and enamels, both pumiceous

and

and pure, accompanied with feltſpars, and the other concomitants with which they are found on the Rock of Burnt Stones; on which account it would be only loſs of time to recapitulate their deſcription. I met with only one new ſtone, which was a common granite, in which were diſtinctly diſcoverable its three conſtituent parts: the feltſpar in ſhining needles; a lightly livid, and ſlightly calcined, quartz; and a black mica, which did not ſhine. It could not therefore be doubted, that it had been expoſed to the action of the fire. But as I found this granite looſe on the ſhore, detached from the volcanic products I have before mentioned, I ſhall notice it no farther.

From the lavas of the horn-ſtone baſe, found on this rock, we obtain, in the furnace, a very compact and hard enamel, which affords ſparks with ſteel; and from the lavas the baſe of which is ſhoerl in the maſs, as alſo from the pumice and the enamel, which originate from the ſame ſtone, is produced a ſcorified enamel, ſo ebullient, that a great part of of it boiled over the edges of the crucible, though it was only half full. This violent fufion, however, produced no fenfible change in the feltfpars.

I fhall conclude this chapter with an obfervation relative to the enamels of the Rock of Burnt Stones, and Procida. They are extremely friable; a flight ftroke with a hammer will break them into pieces; whereas the enamels of moft other volcanos, as we fhall fee in their refpective places, poffefs confiderable hardnefs, and a much greater than that of common glafs. I imagine this defect may be caufed by the feawater, which is mixed with them, and raifed from the fea by the action of fire and aëriform fluids. Thus we know, that thofe liquid vitreous fubftances which are congealed and confolidated in water, are much more friable than when hardened in the air. I am confirmed in this opinion by obferving, that a number of cracks and fiffures are to be found in thefe enamels, an appearance we likewife obferve in glafs which has been

dropped

dropped into water while in a state of fusion. It is to be remarked that these enamels, while they were fluid, have received within them several extraneous bodies; as pieces of tufa and lava, sands and earths of various kinds, which are found within them more or less calcined.

It is probable, from the small distance between Procida and the Rock of Burnt Stones, that they once were joined, and have been separated, in the course of a long series of years, by the action of the sea.

CHAP.

CHAP. V.

ISCHIA.

The castle of Ischia founded on a rock of lava and tufa—Singular species of swallows, which make their nests at its top, and on the higher eminences of the island—Lava of the Arso described—Its pumices originate from the horn-stone—The opinion of some volcanic naturalists, that the lava of the Arso, which flowed in 1302, still smokes, ill founded—Lavas and pumices scattered between the city of Ischia and the Arso—Conical mountain, called the Rotaro, composed of lavas and pumices—Is the only one in the island which contains enamels—The high mountain of St. Niccola, probably, at first, rose out of the sea—Volcanic substances of that mountain—Some of those substances yield sulphate of alumine (alum)—Excursion round the shore of Ischia—
Volcanic

Volcanic productions found there—Ferrugineous sand abundant on that island—Is found to be all crystallized—Enquiries concerning its origin—No prismatic configuration in the lavas which fall into the sea—The assertion of some modern writers, that the lavas of the shores of Ischia are a nidus for the pholades, greatly to be doubted—The Stoves of Ischia, the only probable indication of a remaining internal conflagration—Considerable diminution of this island—Difference between the volcanic materials of Ischia and those of the other Phlegrean Fields—Singular property of the feltspars of the Ischian lavas, which melt in a glass furnace, whereas those of other lavas are almost always infusible by its heat.

THE volcanic substances of which this island, eighteen miles in circuit, is internally composed, prove, beyond the possibility of doubt, that it owes its origin to fire. The obscure epochs of the eruptions of these substances have been fixed, by conjecture, by M. Niccola

Niccola Andria, the learned Profeſſor Royal in the Univerſity of Naples, in his intereſting work, entitled, *Delle Acque Termali**, in which, before he treats of the warm ſprings of Iſchia, he gives a detail of the natural hiſtory of the country, in which he diſplays equal learning and ingenuity. To this work I refer the curious reader, who will find it extremely inſtructive.

I ſhall, however, according to the plan I originally propoſed to myſelf, proceed to deſcribe the principal productions of this iſland which owe their origin to fire, adding ſuch remarks as the ſubject may ſeem to render neceſſary. I ſhall begin therefore at the caſtle of the city of Iſchia, which is built on a rock ſurrounded by the ſea, and a little more than a quarter of a mile in circuit. Lava and tufa are the two component ſubſtances of this rock. The former is different in its appearance, according to the different places in which it is found; but its qualities appeared to me to be ſubſtantially the ſame. Its baſe

* On the waters of hot baths.

is horn-ftone: it is compact, of a moderate hardnefs, an earthy appearance; of a black colour externally, but greyifh within. Its dead lurid hue is diverfified by a few fparkling rhomboidal feltfpars.

The furnace produced from it a very compact enamel, of a mixed colour, between that of honey and dark blue, without any alteration in the feltfpars.

The tufa has no quality by which it is diftinguifhed from the common.

On examining the direction of the tufa and the lava, it was found to continue the fame in the neighbouring mountain, which is feparated from the rock by a narrow channel of the fea: whence it is obvious to infer, that feveral currents have defcended from the mountain and plunged into the water, thus forming the rock, which has been divided from the ifland by the action of the waves.

A number of black and white fwallows

lows* make their nests in different parts of this castle, and in the clefts of the rock. The steep and lofty rocks of the island, likewise, afford a secure retreat to these birds of passage.

Leaving the castle and the city of Ischia, and proceeding about a mile to the west, we meet with a torrent of lava, called the *Arso*, (or Burnt Ground) which is the most recent of any in the island, since it flowed in 1302, and is described by Villani, in his History of —— Florence. It extended about half a mile in breadth, and about a mile and a half in length, and would have flowed farther, had it not met the sea, in which it was buried. The course of the torrent appears interrupted by eminences and descents, and, at some distance, presents to the eye the resemblance of an immense number of large heaps of mulberries confusedly thrown together. It has no visible crater, if by that term we understand, as is usual, a mouth more or less enlarged towards the edges, and contracted

* Hirundo melba. Lin.

at the bottom; for the lava issued from a narrow cleft, at the foot of Mount Tripeta. Though it is little less than five centuries since this lava flowed, a gloomy sterility reigns upon it; it does not produce a single blade of grass, and only affords, in some places, a few arid and useless plants of the lichen, or liverwort. On the surface, and for a little depth, it is light and spungy, and easily crumbles; but, deeper, it becomes dense and harder. The same is observable in many lavas, and is the natural effect of the laws of gravity: the lighter parts of a liquid mass rising to the surface, and the heavier sinking to the bottom.

This lava is of the horn-stone base, and has an earthy ground. Its colour is different in different places, and varies from that of iron to a reddish black. The feltspars incorporated in it are extremely numerous, and, when attentively examined, in some specimens, may induce us to conclude that the fire which produced this torrent must have been extremely violent; since we find the feltspars more or less melted; though,
generally,

generally, those included in lavas appear not to have undergone the least alteration. When we take the lava of the Arso from some depth, in the middle of the current, we find this fusion of the feltspars extremely apparent. Some appear transformed into little globes, or cylinders; others have been only melted on one side, on which they have lost their crystallized form, though they have preserved it entire in other parts. In some cavities of the lava, where the fusion of the feltspars has been more considerable, we meet with singular appearances, which well deserve notice. Sometimes the melted feltspar hangs, as it were, in the air, attached only by some radiating threads of the lava itself, in the centre of which it hangs; while another, melting in the side of a cavity, takes the shape of a transparent concave veil. Even those that have not undergone fusion exhibit decisive signs of a strong calcination. They are extremely friable, and their shining changeable colour is in many places turned to a dead white. In consequence of this calcination, the cystals are often no longer found entire, but fcattered in fmall fragments in the body of the lava. Thofe in the lava on the fides of the current are lefs injured, and their cryftallization is in quadrangular faces.

As the volcanic fire had reduced many of the feltfpars in this lava to a ftate of fufion, I determined to try what effect I could produce on them in the furnace; but though I kept them there two days, I could only obtain a fimple calcination.

M. Dolomieu, fpeaking of the ifland of Ifchia, tells us, that the eruption of the Arfo, though we know it continued two years, never produced any pumice, but only black fcoriæ *. It is true, I could only find fcoriaceous lava on the furface, and folid lava in the internal parts, through the whole length of the courfe of the torrent, except at the aperture whence it had flowed; where, amidft a great quantity of fragments of lava, I

---

* Catalogue Raifonnée des Produits de l'Etna.

found several pieces of pumice, so completely characterised, that there was no danger of confounding them with the light and porose scoriæ, which have been frequently, by persons of insufficient discernment, taken for pumices. These, besides being dry and rough to the touch, were fibrous, with long fibres, vitreous, extremely light, shining, and brittle; whereas the texture of the scoriæ and scoriaceous lava of the Arso is granulous, or so confused that no shadow of a fibre appears; nor have they much friability. In other respects, these pumices of the Arso agree in substance with the scoriæ and lava of the same place: the feltspars in them are alike, and equally affected by the fire. This observation proves, therefore, that the horn-stone, by a violent fire, may be changed into a true pumice, though this transmutation rarely happens.

The above-mentioned French naturalist likewise asserts, that the lava of the Arso still smokes in many places; and that the white fumes which arise from it are very visible

visible in the morning when much dew has fallen.

This assertion, though it must appear somewhat extraordinary, would certainly merit belief had M. Dolomieu himself been an eye-witness to the fact; which had he been, he certainly would have told us. As, however, he only expresses himself in general terms, it is probable he relied on the information of others. The Abbé Breiflak and myself made our observations on the Arso, at the most proper time for discovering these fumes. We repaired thither at sun-rise, and passed there the greatest part of a morning in which there was no want of dew; but our eyes sought this wonderful appearance in vain. Nor could we learn that it had been seen by any other persons; those, at least, of the inhabitants of the vicinity whom we interrogated on the subject, and they were not few, nor people likely to deceive us, all declared that they had never seen either smoke, vapour or mist, arise from the Arso. However, notwithstanding

standing this, I will not take upon me abfolutely to deny the fact. I will only fay, that I find it difficult to overcome my doubts: nor am I convinced by the inftances adduced, by M. Dolomieu, of fome lavas of Etna which have not yet ceafed to fmoke, though they were ejected in 1762; fince the time elapfed in the latter cafe is only twenty-fix years, but in the other four hundred and eighty-fix.

On my return to the city of Ifchia, I met with three lavas rifing from the earth like huge rocks. The bafe of all the three was the horn-ftone, but they were diftinguifhed from each other by certain exterior characters.

One of them was of a cinereous colour, of a coarfe grain, but compact, dry, and rough to the touch. In its external appearance it was not unlike to fome fand-ftones.

The fecond was of a ground entirely earthy: its compactnefs, weight, and hardnefs were, however, greater than thofe of the firft lava.

The

The third, in its recent fractures, was half vitreous; gave sparks with steel, but languidly; and was more fixed, heavy, and hard, than the two others.

All these three lavas had an argillaceous scent, and contained numerous feltspars so brilliant and perfect that they appeared to have entirely eluded the violence of the fire.

A number of detached pumices accompanied these lavas, which they resembled in their general qualities: they contained feltspars and shoerls, but both reduced to a beginning state of fusion.

But no part of the island so abounds with pumices as the Rotaro, a mountain situated between Casamicciola and the city of Ischia. This mountain is of a conical shape, and composed of tufa, pumices, and enamels. It appears to have been produced by a thick and slimy eruption, and is divided into several strata, particularly distinguishable in the road called *Via del Rotaro*. Between these strata

strata there is an immense quantity of pumices, differing in their size, colours, and density; but similar in their texture, which in all is fibrous. They contain various feltspars, which manifest a beginning fusion. They do not form continued currents, as we observe in many of the pumices of Lipari, but are found in detached pieces; yet so disposed, that, in many places, they form beds or strata. It appears extremely probable, that the volcano, after an eruption of tufa, threw up a shower of pumices, which falling on the tufa produced a bed or stratum, upon which another eructation formed another tufaceous stratum, that was again covered with another shower of pumices; and thus, by alternate ejections of tufaceous and pumiceous matters, a great part of the conical mountain was formed. The extent of the pumices, in the direction of the *Via del Rotaro*, is more than a mile; and they principally abound in the more elevated places, where those most proper for the purposes for which these stones are used in Italy, may be collected in great abundance.

Intermixed with the pumices and tufa, we find many pieces of enamel, the thickness of which is from an inch to a foot and a half, and even two feet. These were probably thrown out at the time when the above-mentioned mountain was formed. They are of a black colour, and yield to the strokes of a hammer much more than the enamels of the Rock of Burnt Stones and Procida. Like them, they abound in felt-spars, and present the usual rhomboidal figure. The Rotaro is the only place in Ischia which affords enamels.

It seems as if it might be considered as an invariable rule, that, among the mountains of different elevation which have given birth to volcanic islands, that which rises above the rest, and is commonly placed in the centre, was first produced by the fire; and that those which surround it, and, by their junction and extent, form the body of the island, are the work of succeeding eruptions, which have issued either from the crater of the primitive mountain, or from the

the lateral and lower craters, whence have been ejected that aggregate of fubaltern and fucceffively lower mountains, by which the moft elevated, which occupies the centre, is furrounded. In this manner, we perceive feveral of the Eolian ifles to have been formed. Such alfo has been the origin of Ifchia; where the mountain of St. Niccola, which in earlier times was called Epopeo, and which is in the centre of the ifland, and higher than the reft, was no doubt the firft that towered above the waves. The conftituent fubftances of this mountain are of various kinds. I have confidered, with fome attention, thofe on the fide of Lacco, which are ftones that, in the fame manner as thofe of Solfatara, have undergone a decompofition, probably to be attributed to fulphureous acids, if from the refemblance of effects we may argue a fimilarity of caufe. The rocks near the fea, on the coaft of Fafano, are lefs decompofed; nor is it difficult to difcover their nature, which is granitous; the mica, feltfpar, and quartz, being clearly difcernible, with fome greenifh particles of fteatites.

steatites. The quartz and feltspars, though somewhat calcined, are tolerably hard; and the mica, which is black, has not lost its native splendour. This rock, which does not appear to have suffered fusion, is whitish, and changed in such a manner that it will not resist a blow of the hammer.

Proceeding towards the summit of the Epopeo, we meet with decomposed lavas, partly of the horn-stone base, and partly of that of the petro silex, in which, however, the argilla occupies no small part. The lavas of this latter quality, in part not affected by the sulphureous acids, are of a black hue, of considerable compactness, give sparks freely with steel, and in their fractures, and sometimes externally, present a siliceous appearance. Their odour is sensibly argillaceous. These petrosiliceous lavas are not simple, but contain within them some small flakes of feltspar and mica.

In the furnace they melt into a substance of the colour and lustre of pitch, in which, however,

however, the white feltspars appear, or rather are conspicuous.

These lavas are found to be variously decomposed by the acids, in the same manner as is observable in those of Solfatara. In some places, they are covered with a thin whitish crust, light, soft to the touch, which attaches to the tongue, and is extremely friable. In others, this crust is some inches deep, and in others, it extends through the whole thickness of the lava. Sometimes we find it so softened that it has become pulverous; and there is a great quantity of white dust on the brow of the mountain. We may therefore conclude that the sulphureous acids have there been very abundant, and of long duration; though now there is no perceivable sign of any such exhalations.

We know that formerly in Ischia the sulphate of alumine (alum) was extracted for commercial purposes; and according to M. Andria, who has been before cited, the manufacture

manufacture of this falt was principally carried on at Catrico, a place fituated above Lacco, on the higher eminences of the Epopeo. He informs us, however, that he was not able, after the moſt careful and minute refearch, to difcover any remaining veſtige of fulphate of alumine. I will candidly ſtate what I myſelf obſerved.

I collected a number of fpecimens of the different lavas of Catrico and the environs. They are generally compact, very white, and homogeneous to the eye; but they differ from each other by the following exterior characters: Some are moderately heavy and hard: in their recent fractures, and frequently without, they are fmooth; and in the centre of fome we find a fmall nucleus of blackifh lava, but little decompofed. Others are very light, may be fcratched by the nail, are rough and fomewhat pulverous in their fractures, and fcarcely ever contain within them any refidue not decompofed. In fhort, the former lavas have undergone lefs change by the fulphureous acids than the latter.

latter. When I first examined, on the spot, the fragments of these two lavas, I could not perceive by the taste any symptom of the sulphate of alumine; but when I had conveyed my specimens to Pavia, together with other volcanic substances, and placed them in my cabinet, on large tables, after some months I observed the following appearances:

In the lavas of Catrico and its vicinity, which had been less affected by the acids, I could discover no trace of alum; but in the other lavas of the same situation, which had been more changed by the said acids, I perceived the sweetish and astringent taste of that salt; and could discover a whitish thin coat of the same, which entirely incrusted them.

At the end of six months the thickness of this coat was a quarter of a line; after which, I did not perceive it to increase in thickness. I made new fractures in these lavas, and continually discovered new coats of the sulphate of alumine; and at the time I now write, which is twenty-seven months since I brought the specimens of lava from Ischia, they still retain a thin saline crust. I have also satisfactorily ascertained the true nature of this sulphate of alumine, by the ordinary chemical proofs.

As to the second species of lava, it never, at any time, exhibited any sign of the presence of this sulphate; nor have I been able to obtain it by calcination, and a method similar to that which is employed in the territory of Civita Vecchia for extracting alum from such argillaceous stones.

These observations, however, sufficiently prove, that this valuable salt might still be obtained at Ischia; nor should it excite surprise that, when on the spot, I could not discover it by the taste; since the humidity of the night, the dew, and still more the rains, had dissipated it as fast as it effloresced. As the species of decomposed lava in which I discovered it is found in very large quantities

quantities on the Epopeo, this branch of commerce, which has been so long neglected in Ischia, might doubtless be revived with very great advantage.

Besides the places I have mentioned, I examined this island in many others, without discovering any novelty worthy of remark; but I could not entirely satisfy myself with such excursions. When I first formed the design of attentively examining Ischia and the other Eolian isles, I resolved not only to make my researches in their interior parts, but to coast their shores in a boat, landing at such places as appeared the most suitable to my enquiries. In this manner I met with many volcanic bodies, which I should have sought in vain within the island; either because they do not exist there, or because they are rendered inaccessible by the rocks and precipices with which they are surrounded, or which they themselves form. The coasts of the volcanic isles are also clothed with lavas, which run out into the sea, and which, in some

some places, by tracing them upwards, discover the crater, or mouth from which they have issued. Lastly, by coasting the shores of the islands, we may be enabled to determine, whether the prismatic lavas owe their origin to the sea; many writers of repute having asserted that the regularity of their form arises from the sudden congelation that takes place on their precipitating into the sea-water, which causes them to take the shape of regular prismatic columns; a configuration which, they affirm, is only found in places adjoining to the sea.

For these reasons I determined, after having examined the higher parts of the island, to proceed to consider the lower; and took my departure from Lacco, by water, coasting the island on the left. The first mountain which presented itself was the Vico, partly formed of tufa, and partly of two currents of lava, which descend into the sea. The colour of the first, which is of a horn-stone base, is between the grey and iron colour: it is of an unequal grain, earthy, moderately hard;

hard; and abounds in feltspars, some in thin plates, others in prisms, and both conspicuous for their brilliancy.

The other lava, which is of the same base, and contains similar feltspars, is less compact, more earthy, and, consequently, less hard: its colour is partly cinereous, and partly grey. These two lavas, in their descent, have raised themselves into little mounts, and are of a considerable thickness.

Farther on is Monte Zaro, formed, towards the sea, by a river of lava extending a mile in length, and nearly two in breadth. It appears to have been generated by several successive eruptions, which have consolidated one after the other. The base of this lava is horn-stone, and it contains mica and feltspars. It is various in its colour, being in some parts of the current of a more or less reddish blue, in others cinereous, and in others white. The mica, which is black, and especially conspicuous in the white pieces,

pieces, though it has not undergone fusion, has lost its lustre, and acquired a much greater degree of friability than it naturally has. The same has not happened to the feltspars, which are as well preserved as if they had never been exposed to the fire. They give sparks plentifully with steel, have a beauteous changeable lustre, are of a vitreous, semitransparent whiteness, and, being broken, are detached with difficulty. This species of lava so abounds with them, that they occupy the full half of its volume. The greater part are prisms.

Another lava makes a part of the same current of Monte Zaro. This, though it is likewise of a horn-stone base, differs from the former by being one third less heavy, and of an earthy appearance; whereas that of the other is somewhat vitreous. Its colour, in the more internal parts, is reddish; but, in the external, an ochreous yellow. On the surface especially it is manifestly decomposed; for it is become so soft that it may be scraped with a knife. But the cause which

which has produced this fuperficial decompofition in the lava has not injured the feltfpars, which are extremely perfect, and, in this lava, may be eafily extracted, to examine their figure, which is hexagonal with rhomboidal faces. Some of them are half an inch in length, though others are not more than a line.

The bottom of Monte Zaro, which is wafhed by the fea, is covered with a vitreous fand; which, viewed with a lens, appears to confift of a number of particles of feltfpars, which by liquefaction have had their angles blunted, and been reduced to a roundifh figure. They belong to the feltfpars of the laft-mentioned lava.

From the termination of Monte Zaro to the beginning of Monte Imperatore is a long and ample tract, almoft entirely tufaceous, fcattered over with *rapillo*, as the Neapolitans call it; or, as a naturalift would fay, with fragments of pumice.

The side of Monte Imperatore which over-hangs the sea, derives its origin from a very singular species of lava. I have already spoken of the abundance of feltspars in the lava of Monte Zaro; but in this they are found so prodigiously numerous, that at first view they appear to constitute the entire substance. It is necessary to break it, and consider the pieces attentively, to perceive that it has a base, which is of a yellowish earthy horn-stone, easily friable, to very small quantities of which the feltspars are feebly attached. Their crystallization is in rhomboidal faces of various sizes, from a line to three quarters of an inch. To this little earthy base are likewise attached various small scales of black hexaedrous mica.

The same Monte Imperatore presents us, on the side of the sea, with large quantities of another lava; which, excepting a very few particles of yellow mica, and some still fewer microscopic feltspars, may be considered as simple. This likewise has for its base the horn-stone. The lava appears to have

have issued from the mouth of the volcano at different times, as we find currents which have flowed over currents, intermixed in a strange and confused manner.

Leaving the Monte Imperatore, we next arrive at the Calle di Panza; a place on the shore, from which rises a very high and large rock of lava, interrupted by some protuberances, that attract the eye at a distance, and invite observation, which they certainly merit, as they consist of beautiful groups of numerous rough rhomboidal feltspars, some two inches in length. They are of a yellowish white, transparent in a slight degree, of a vitreous appearance, a changing aspect, a foliating texture, and manifest their hardness by the quantity of sparks they give with steel. Many hundreds of them, grouped together, form roundish masses of half a foot, a foot, and two feet in thickness, which at their lower extremity are set in the lava. Though, as has been said, they are very hard; yet, by the means of certain fissures they contain, they may easily

be

be divided into small pieces, either of the parallelopipedon or rhomboidal form. Whence it appears that they have been injured by some external agent, but which seems to have had no relation to sulphureous acid vapours, as we do not perceive the smallest indication of these, either in the feltspars, or in the lava which contains them. This agent, however, whatever it may have been, has produced a considerable effect on the lava, which is corroded in every part; and it is in consequence of its being so deeply corroded, that the groups of feltspars have been left uncovered, so that they may easily, with an iron point, be extracted entire.

This fact appeared to me the more deserving of remark, as in all my former volcanic researches I had never met with any similar: nor indeed have I since; the feltspars of other lavas being never grouped, or forming a kind of tumours, but scattered, and distributed within them in equal quantities. But in what manner are we to consider these tumours? Are they extraneous
bodies

bodies that have been by accident included within the lava while it was in a fluid state? This is possible; but it appears to me much more natural to suppose that they appertained to the stony substance which has been changed into lava by the violence of the fire. I would, therefore, thus explain this phenomenon. Since, as we have already observed, the feltspars (and the same may be affirmed of the shoerls) are not the produce or consequence of the fire, as they are found to exist in many of the primordial rocks; it appears most probable that they were formed within those rocks when they were in a state of fluidity, or at least sufficiently approaching it. I mean to say, that then the integrant particles of the feltspars, by their powerful affinity, united in crystallized masses. Where they were at a certain distance from each other, they united, forming complete crystals; but where they were thickly clustered, their tumultuary union produced groups of crystals, the greater part of which were of irregular forms. The same may be observed in salts, stones, and especially

cially in quartzofe and fparry cryftals. Thus, with refpect to the feltfpars in this lava: they are contained in every part of it; and, where there is any fpace interpofed between them, their cryftallization is perfect; but very imperfect in the groups I have defcribed, and probably from the caufe fuggefted above.

This lava, like the preceding, has for its bafe the horn-ftone; and the external appearance of its current refembles that of a ftream which, precipitating from a height, has been fuddenly congealed and hardened by cold. It abounds, therefore, in inequalities, elevations, and defcents; and, on obferving its principal track, which paffes by the Calle di Panza, we are led to expect that the aperture whence it flowed lies higher, in the direction of that place, where it is in fact found.

A ftrong wind rifing from the fouth, though it did not prevent me from coafting the ifland, hindered me from landing,
as

as there was danger of being dashed on some rock by the violence of the waves. I could therefore only observe at a distance a variety of lavas, and a great quantity of tufa, which, being continually beaten and diminished by the waves, form precipices, and cliffs, hanging over the sea.

I however continued my researches by removing to the northern side of the island, where I was sheltered from the wind; but I did not find that the volcanic productions to be met with here presented any novelty. They were almost all of the horn-stone base, and filled, as usual, with crystallized feltspars.

I did not fail to collect and examine the sand of the other parts of the island where I landed, as well as that of the shore near Monte Zaro. I found it, as I expected, to be of the same nature with the volcanic productions at the foot of which it was found. The greater portion of the sand consisted, however, of small fragments of feltspars;

feltspars; that being the stone which most abounds in these lavas, and which best resists the vicissitudes of the seasons, and every extrinsic injury.

I must not omit to mention the ferrugineous sand which we meet with in many parts of the island, and which is especially abundant on the sea shore. It not only moves the magnetic needle, but is strongly attracted by the loadstone. This sand is well known in Naples, and other places; but one of its qualities, which I discovered with the assistance of a lens, has not, to my knowledge, been hitherto observed. At the first view I imagined, with the generality of naturalists, that it must consist of very minute particles of iron, of entirely irregular shape, like those of lapidarious sands. Such, in fact, they appeared to the naked eye; but, by the aid of a good lens, I discovered, with pleasing surprise, that every grain was the fragment of a crystal, or a complete crystal, of native iron. Of the latter there were not more than three or four among every

every hundred grains. Thefe fmall martial cryftals are formed of two quadrangular pyramids united at the bafe, and every fide of the pyramid is a rectangular or ifofceles triangle. But, in general, we meet with only the fragment of a cryftal, and perceive that the part wanting has been deftroyed by the action of the waves of the fea on the ferrugineous fand; many of the grains exhibiting their angles blunted, and having affumed a globofe figure.

This fand is not confined to Ifchia; it is likewife found, in confiderable quantities, on the fhore of Pozzuolo. But what is its origin? It is certain that this iron could not thus have cryftallized without having a bafe, or point of fupport; and, in the volcanized countries, no fubftance prefents itfelf more proper for fuch a bafe than the lava, on and within which it has affumed this configuration: but it muft be allowed that this lava has been deftroyed by length of time, fince, among the innumerable fpecimens I have obferved in thefe countries, I have
not

not found one which exhibited similar martial crystals.

While making the circuit of this island, I continually had in my recollection the opinion of those naturalists who, as I have mentioned above, maintain that the formation of prismatic lavas owes its origin to the sudden immersion of the flowing lava into the water. I could not have wished a better opportunity to form a judgment on this hypothesis, than I here found; where a multitude of currents of lava, in different directions, appear to have rushed into the sea, in which they are still visible to a considerable depth. But I did not meet with one that had assumed any such regular form, or any other resembling it; either among the lavas above the water, those which touch its surface in their descent, or those immersed within it, as far at least as the eye could discern.

From the observations I made while coasting this little island, I was likewise strongly

strongly induced to doubt of a fact expressly asserted by M. Andria, in these words: " The lavas, in some places near the sea shore, are found full of holes made by the pholades; at least I am of opinion they are to be attributed to those animals, though I could not find in them any fragments of their shells."

He then immediately proceeds to reason on this fact. " It is manifest that the pholades were directed by instinct to make their lodgments here; but they could not do this till after a long time, when the lava was become fixed and solid."

I shall not venture expressly to contradict this assertion, as I was not able to examine the whole shore of Ischia; and, even if I had examined it, I should still have distrusted my researches; since I could not have been certain that I had explored the precise places of which he speaks, as they are not distinctly described. I shall only candidly say, that I greatly fear there is some mistake,

mistake, since I never met with any lavas, or other volcanic substances, which had been made the habitation of the pholas, whether by that name he understands the *mytilus lithophagus*, or the *pholas dactylus* of Linnæus. In my researches relative to marine animals, I have given particular attention to those which pierce and inhabit sub-aqueous stones. I have examined, with the utmost care, the volcanic substances of Etna, which are bathed by the sea, those of the Eolian isles, and some of those of Vesuvius. Nothing is more frequent than to find on these, various kinds of testaceous animals, as oysters, serpules, lepades, and various others of the same species; but I never found them pierced by pholades, or any other animals which corrode fossil substances. I have found these animals in places not volcanic, though not in all, as I have observed that they never make their lodgements but in calcareous stones, of which kind the Ischian lavas, and, in general, other lavas, are not. I therefore incline to suspect that some other cavities, resembling those

those which are the work of the pholades, have deceived M. Andria. I could at least wish that he would ascertain the fact by repeating his observations on the spot, as, should it be established, it would, in my opinion, be the only example of the kind ever discovered in volcanized stones.

I employed three days in examining this island; and, during my researches, carefully observed whether I could discern any smoke or vapour arising from the ground, whence it might be concluded that the volcanic conflagrations were not entirely extinguished; but I could not discover the least appearance of the kind, nor had any been observed by the oldest inhabitants of the vicinity, of whom I made the most careful enquiries. The stoves of Ischia may, however, induce us to be of a contrary opinion. It is well known that these stoves are filled with warm aqueous vapours; which continually issue from cracks and fissures in the lava, and which, though they have some of the noxious qualities common to volcanic exhalations,

exhalations, are extremely beneficial in many diforders. Thefe certainly can only be produced by a heat which, whatever may be the caufe of it, raifes the fubterraneous water in vapour.

This ifland, when it was firft produced by conflagrations in ancient, and, to us, unknown times, muft have been of much greater extent than it is at prefent. The fouthern fide, expofed to a fea which beats againft it without any interpofing obftacle, and formed in many places of tufa, one of the leaft hard of volcanic fubftances, muft have been confiderably worn away and diminifhed; and this diminution muft continually increafe. Time, which changes and deftroys every thing, has likewife produced a great alteration in the interior parts of the ifland. From the fummit of Epopeo, we difcover a number of conical eminences; but their internal craters no longer exift, nor do we find in Ifchia inconteftible traces of a fingle one, fince thofe depths and ample cavities, thofe refem-
blances

blances of theatres and amphitheatres, which we obferve around us, may be equally the effect of fire or water.

I fhall conclude thefe obfervations by an important reflection on the volcanic materials of Ifchia. Thefe are different from thofe of the other Phlegrean fields. Except the mountain Vefuvius, the extenfive plain on which the city of Naples ftands, the furrounding hills to the north, the northweft, and the weft, the craters of the lakes Agnano and Averno, many parts of Solfatara, Monte Nuovo, the promontory of Mifeno, Procida, &c. they are the refult of tufaceous fubftances. Thefe are, in fact, not wanting in Ifchia; but the predominant part of its compofition is various kinds of rock, and principally the horn-ftone. The eruption of the Arfo, likewife, which is the laft conflagration of which we have any knowledge, is compofed of the fame ftone. The fubftances, therefore, which have furnifhed aliment to the different conflagrations of Ifchia, have had their centre in thofe argillaceous rocks,

rocks, which by the above-mentioned eruption in 1302 shewed that they were not then exhausted.

These rocks, as we have seen, abound in crystallized feltspars, which, in the furnace, exhibit a quality we rarely meet with in the feltspars of other lavas subjected to the same degree of heat. I mean their fusibility. If we except those of the Arso, which do not yield to the fire, all the feltspars of these lavas may be perfectly liquefied. The lava, in which the feltspars are contained, acquires a clear colour, and becomes slightly transparent; while in other parts it presents an opaque and imperfect enamel. If the quantity of the feltspars included is more than double that of the lava, the product which results is a true glass, but somewhat less transparent than factitious glass; but when the feltspars are solitary, and not at all injured by the lava, like those of the Calle di Panza, the glass is perfect and extremely transparent. It has no colour, is very compact, and gives sparks strongly with steel.

To

To bring it to this perfection, it requires a fire of about two days. At the end of the firſt day, the feltſpar is only reduced to a paſte, ſimilar to porcelain; the pieces then conglutinate together; many exhibit a ſemi-vitrification, and the ſurface within the crucible is not horizontal and even, but has riſings and cavities, according as the pieces have been put in: by continuing the fire, however, it becomes level and ſmooth.

The proſecution of theſe experiments induced me to attempt to fuſe, with the ſame degree of heat, two other feltſpars which are not from volcanic countries; the one being from Mount St. Gothard, and the other from Baveno. Father Pini has the honour of their diſcovery. The firſt is in maſs, of a ſhining white, foliated, and very hard. I kept it in the furnace during eight-and-forty hours, but it had only contracted a ſlight ſuperficial vitreous appearance. When placed within two crucibles joined by their tops, with charcoal entirely ſurrounding them, in a furnace, the fire of which was violently excited by the bellows

bellows for two hours, the angles of this feltſpar became blunted, and the pieces attached together, contracting a ſmooth ſurface, and a milky whiteneſs, but without any ſenſible fuſion taking place in the internal parts.

The other feltſpar, from Baveno, is cryſtallized in tetrahedrous priſms, opaque, leſs hard than the former, and of a reddiſh yellow colour. After continuing forty-eight hours in the furnace, a ſlight conglutination took place in the pieces, which had acquired a ſnowy whiteneſs.

On comparing theſe two feltſpars and others contained in innumerable lavas, with thoſe of the Iſchian lavas, we may conclude that it is very rarely that the fuſion of theſe ſtones can be obtained by the utmoſt heat of a glaſs furnace.

From theſe obſervations on the lavas of Iſchia we likewiſe learn another truth. Mineralogiſts have ſaid that ſhoerls are more eaſily eafily fufible than feltfpars; becaufe they have obferved that the degree of heat in which the former fufe is infufficient to fufe the latter. But I have experienced that this affertion is not always true; and it will be feen in the courfe of this work, that the fhoerls of fome lavas will refift the fame degree of heat in which the feltfpars of Ifchia are completely fufed. The caufe of this may be, either that the filex fometimes is lefs abundant in the feltfpars than in the fhoerls, or that their component principles are proportioned in fuch a manner, that the fufion of fome is facilitated more than that of others, or becaufe they contain more iron, it being well known that this metal promotes the fufion of ftones.

CHAP.

CHAP. VI.

THE VALLEY OF METELONA, NEAR CASERTA.

The tufa found in this valley, composed of fragments of pumice surrounded by calcareous earths—Pieces of enamel mixed with it—This tufa different from other volcanic tufas—Probability that it communicates with the volcanos of Naples and its environs, and perhaps also with those of the Agro Romano and Tuscany—Means proposed to ascertain whether the Bay of Naples be the remains of an ancient volcanic crater, and to what distance within the sea the roots of Mount Vesuvius and those of Ischia extend.

AN excursion from Naples to Caserta, and thence to the neighbouring aqueducts, furnished me with an opportunity for new volcanic

canic obfervations. Some miles before we arrive at the fmall city of Caferta, ennobled by the fuperb royal palace, which may be faid to confift of four grand palaces united in one by the hand of a mafter, we meet with calcareous earth, which continues to the aqueducts, diftant fix miles from that city, and which are a prodigy of art. They confift of a large and magnificent bridge, of the aftonifhing length of two miles, and of a proportionate breadth. Within this bridge runs a wide canal, brought from a mountain at the diftance of twenty-fix miles, which, paffing through fubterranean conduits, fkirts the fide of the hill, and defcends to Caferta, near the Royal Gardens. As the neighbouring mountains abound in calcareous ftone, I was not furprifed to find the pavement of the bridge formed of that ftone; but it fomewhat excited my attention when I perceived that the remainder of the edifice was conftructed with volcanic tufa, in which are mixed fome pieces of enamel. Sir William Hamilton has told us, that in the environs of Caferta, below a ftratum of vegetable

table earth four or five feet in thickness, we meet with cinders, pumices, and fragments of lava; and that, on digging near the foundations of the above-mentioned aqueducts, volcanic earths are difcovered. I therefore firft conjectured that the tufa had been procured from thefe fubterranean places; an opinion in which I was confirmed by obferving that the whole country round was calcareous, not excepting the higheft mountains, which were, nearly all, of the fame contexture and colour with the chains of hills between Naples and Loretto. One of the inhabitants of this part of the country, however, aſſured me that this tufa was dug from a plain, about a mile diſtant to the north, called the *Valley of Metelona,* of which I was convinced, on repairing to the fpot. This tufa, in feveral places, lies in heaps on each fide of the public road, principally near the *Taverna,* where we find the excavations, not within but above the ground, which have in part fupplied materials for thefe aqueducts. This tufa is extremely porous, and being immerfed in water attracts it forcibly, and

and with a flightly hiffing found, as is the cafe with other bibacious bodies. Like tufas in general, it has a moderate weight and confiftence, is rough to the touch, and inclines to a yellow colour. But, on a more minute examination, it difcovers its original, and is found to be compofed of a mixture of fmall fragments of pumice, and any piece of it detached from the mafs will be found to contain fragments of that ftone. It appears as if compofed of fmall threads extended lengthwife, which viewed with the lens are found to be flender filaments, extremely friable, and generally parallel to each other. It contains many cavities, within which the pumice appears changed into vitreous balls; we likewife find little globes of pumice, which have an external vitreous coat, but which, within, have preferved their fibrous nature: laftly, in fome parts of this tufa are contained pieces of folid enamel, extremely friable, fhining, and in their fractures refembling afphaltum.

The tufa now defcribed is of a fingular quality;

quality; at least, in my travels through the Two Sicilies, I have not found any resembling it. The others are, usually, of an argillaceous base; this, as has been said, is a composition of fragments of pumice. Hence we may easily conceive that the results produced by the furnace must be different. The tufa of Metelona afforded a true enamel, but the others remained infusible.

The edges of the tufa, or rather of the broken and half pulverized pumices, are surrounded with calcareous stone. There is, however, no doubt that these pumices, besides having deep roots, extend likewise laterally among the stone to a great distance. These volcanic matters have probably an immediate communication with the volcanos of Naples and its environs, as also with those of the Agro Romano, and perhaps also with those of Tuscany, so as to form a soil entirely volcanized, of immense extent.

Some have conjectured, and perhaps not without reason, that the great bason of the
sea,

sea, called the bay of Naples, in front of Capri, is the remains of an ancient volcanic crater. It would contribute to the advancement of natural knowledge, were the bottom to be explored, at various distances from the shore, by the means of such instruments as are employed to fish up coral, and, sometimes, pieces of the rock on which it grows. Should we by such means discover a cavity similar to an inverted funnel, or draw up substances from the bottom, which should be known to owe their origin to fire, this conjecture would become a well-founded opinion.

A portion of the roots of Mount Vesuvius are bathed by the sea. Who can say how far these roots may extend under the water? The same may be remarked of Ischia, which, perhaps, as some have conjectured, was anciently joined to Procida: it were to be wished that we could obtain facts that might ascertain the truth of such conjectures. It is well known how far Sir William Hamilton has extended the limits of the volcanization

zation of the Phlegrean fields, by land; and there is no doubt but they might be still more enlarged by sea. The experiments necessary for this are certainly difficult, but not impossible. The industry of two Italians of merit, the Count Ferdinando Marsigli, and Vitaliano Donati, has made us acquainted with the nature of the bottom of some parts of the Mediterranean, and the Adriatic. In the course of this work I shall state what I have observed relative to the bottom of the famous strait of Messina, and that in which the channels that separate the Eolian isles terminate. It is greatly to be wished, for the advancement of volcanic knowledge, that the bottom of the sea near Naples, and the adjacent places, might be explored by similar experiments.

CHAP.

CHAP. VII.

JOURNEY TO MOUNT ETNA.

Comparison between Vesuvius and Etna—The lavas of the latter volcano begin to appear, from the sea, at the distance of thirty-seven miles from Messina—Different epochs of the flowing of these lavas—Modern Catania almost entirely built of lava; as was the ancient city, which was destroyed by an earthquake in 1693—Remarks on the observations of Mr. Brydone, relative to Etna —Uncertainty of the opinion of Count Borch, that the age of the lava may be calculated by the quantity of vegetable earth produced by time—Fruitless attempts to render cultivable the eruption of 1669—The thinness of the crust of vegetable earth, the cause of the fertility of the lower region of Etna— Monte Rosso—Eructation of its lavas— Abundance of shoerls on this mountain— Chemical

Chemical analysis of these shoerls—Feltspars not always more difficult to fuse than shoerls—View from Monte Rosso of the whole current which, in 1669, flowed into the sea—Calamities suffered, at different times, by St. Niccolo dell Arena from the eruptions of Etna—Lavas of the middle region—Its great celebrity for luxuriant vegetation, and the loftiness of its trees—Great antiquity of these two regions—Grotta delle Capre—Nature of the lavas of that grotto.

THOUGH Vesuvius, considered in itself, may be justly called a grand volcano, and though, from the destruction and calamities it has at various times occasioned, it has continually been an object of consternation and terror to the inhabitants of the neighbouring country; yet when it is compared with Etna it must lose much of its celebrity, and appear so diminished, that, if the expression may be allowed, it may be called a volcano for a cabinet. Vesuvius does not, perhaps, rise higher than a mile above the level of the sea; and the whole circuit of its base,

including

including Ottajano and Somma, is not more than thirty miles; while Mount Etna covers a space of one hundred and eighty, and in its height above the sea considerably exceeds two miles. From the sides of Etna other lesser mountains rise, which are as it were its offspring, and more than one of which equals Vesuvius in size. The most extensive lavas of the latter mountain do not exceed seven miles in length; while those of Etna are fifteen or twenty, and some even thirty miles in extent. The borders of the crater of Mount Etna are never less than a mile in circuit, and, according to the changes to which they are subject, sometimes two or three miles; it is even reported, that in the dreadful eruption of 1669 they were enlarged to six [*]. But the circumference of the Vesuvian crater is never more than half a mile, even when widest distended, in its most destructive conflagrations [†]. Lastly, the earthquakes occasioned

---

[*] Borelli, Hist. Incend. Ætnæ, an. 1669.

[†] I know not how M. Sage was led into so strange an error as to assert that *the crater of Vesuvius is more than*

sioned by the two volcanos, their eruptions, showers of ignited stones, and the destruction and desolation they occasion, are all likewise proportionate to their respective dimensions. We cannot therefore wonder that visits to Vesuvius should be considered as undertakings of little consequence, and never be made public, except lavas should have been flowing at the time; while a journey to Etna is considered as no trivial enterprise, both from the difficulty of the way, and the distance; as from Catania, whence it is usual to set out, it is thirty miles to the summit of Etna. On such a journey, likewise, we have to pass through three different climates; whereas to go from Naples to Vesuvius should be rather called an excursion than a journey. We find also little difference between the temperature of the air at the bottom of this latter mountain, and that of its summit. Notwithstanding these difficulties, however, the

---

than three miles in diameter. (Elem. de Min. tom. 1.) Were this true, the circumference of the Vesuvian crater must be nearly ten miles, an extent which perhaps the crater of no volcano in the world ever had.

gigantic

gigantic majefty of the Sicilian volcano, its fublime elevation, and the extenfive, varied, and grand profpects its fummit prefents, have induced the curious, in every age, to afcend and examine it; and not a few have tranfmitted to pofterity the obfervations they have made during their arduous journey.

Thefe examples would alone have ftrongly excited me to make the fame journey, and fimilar refearches; but I had alfo a ftill more powerful incentive in the undertaking in which I had engaged to travel through the Two Sicilies, in order to make obfervations on the volcanos, among which Etna muft principally claim my attention, as being the largeft and moft ftupendous of all that are, at prefent, in a ftate of conflagration on the furface of the globe. I was, likewife, induced to believe that, notwithftanding fo many journeys to this mountain have already appeared, I might ftill publifh mine; and that for feveral reafons. Firft, becaufe I flatter myfelf that I fhall be able to ftate fome obfervations which will be, in part at leaft, new to the reader; secondly, because I shall thus have an opportunity to examine many things related by the travellers who have preceded me, which do not always appear to bear the stamp of truth; and lastly, because my remarks may furnish subjects for useful discussion.

I took my departure from Messina for Catania, a distance of sixty miles, by sea, in a small vessel, coasting close upon the land, all the way, to examine the shore. On the 1st of September, I landed, at the distance of fifteen miles from Messina, on a part of the shore which forms there a head-land, where mariners are accustomed, sometimes, to make a short stay. The shore here was entirely of calcareous earth, except some pieces of scattered detached lava. The latter production excited in me some doubts whether the explosions of Etna had ever reached to so great a distance; but the mariners who were with me assured me, that these pieces of lava had been brought from the shore of Catania by vessels who had taken them in as ballast, and left them

them here when they had no farther occafion for them, in confequence of having taken in other lading. Of the truth of this account I was afterwards fatisfied, as I found this lava perfectly fimilar to that in the neighbourhood of Catania.

The real eruptions of this volcano begin firft to appear, in the form of rocks of different elevations, which overhang the fea, at the diftance of thirty-feven miles from Meffina, on the way to Catania; and at the fame diftance Etna is faintly feen to fmoke, and majeftically raifes its head above the other mountains of Sicily. We had a clear view of it, the fky being free from clouds; and I began to entertain a hope that I fhould be able to vifit its higheft fummit, fince it was not, as it frequently is, covered with fnow.

Before we arrived at Catania, I landed at feveral places, to examine the fhore, which is entirely formed of lava. I was particularly attentive to its courfe and changeable ftructure. The greater part of the lavas proceed in a right line from the body of Mount Etna, with various inclinations to the level of the sea; and many of them, having been broken by the violent shocks of the waves, exhibit their various stratification, and shew the different epochs in which they have flowed, by the difference of their strata, and the coatings of vegetable earth more or less thick interspersed between those strata.

All these lavas, at least those which I examined, are similar with respect to their base, as they all derive their origin from the hornstone, and all contain within them feltspar cryſtals.

I employed two days in this coasting voyage from Messina to Catania. The materials of which the latter city is built are such as might be expected in a volcanized country, where stones of any other than a volcanic nature are not to be found but at a considerable distance. The edifices, both public and private, and even the walls of the city, are principally of lava; which has furnished

nished materials not only for the modern Catania, but also for that more ancient city, which was entirely destroyed by an earthquake in the year 1693; at least its ruins when dug up have all been found to consist of lava. We learn likewise from observations anterior to that fatal period, that lava has been met with under its foundations on the occasion of digging for wells*; nor is it possible for us to say to what depth the roots of the Etnean eruptions extend. If we only take a view of the surface of the territory of Catania, we every where meet with immense accumulations of lava, among which the most conspicuous are the remains of that torrent which poured from one of the sides of Etna in 1669, inundated, with wide-spreading ruin, a space of fourteen miles in length, and nearly four in breadth, rose over the walls of Catania, burying under it a part of the city, and at length precipitated itself into the sea.

It would be a superfluous labour were I to

* Borelli, ubi sup.

proceed

proceed to give a long and minute description of this torrent of lava, which has been already so amply described by Mr. Brydone*, Count Borch †, Sir William Hamilton ‡, and Riedesel §; though I cannot say that the relations of four travellers, who repeat the same things after each other, were much wanted; since our illustrious countryman, the Italian Alphonsus Borelli, who was present at the time when this dreadful torrent of fire burst forth, wrote a work expressly to describe it ‖. It appears to me preferable to

---

* Tour through Sicily. † Lettres sur la Sicile.

‡ Campi Phlegræi. § Travels in Sicily.

‖ Mr. Brydone is the only one of these travellers who mentions Borelli. He cites four observations from him; but perverts them, to give them more an air of the marvellous.

He says, first, that according to the testimony of Borelli, " after the most violent struggles and shakings " of the whole island, when the lava at last burst " through, it sprang up into the air to the height of " sixty palms."

Mr. Brydone I hope will pardon me, when I tell him that Borelli, here, certainly, only speaks of some local shocks, and tremblings of certain places in the vicinity of

to prefent the reader with the view, with fome improvement which this celebrated Phyfician of the volcano, and by no means of a fhaking felt over the whole ifland. As for the lava fpringing up into the air to the height of fixty palms, there is not a word about it in the whole book.

Mr. Brydone, likewife, makes Borelli fay, that " for " many weeks the fun did not appear, and the day " feemed to be changed into night."

But all we find in Borelli's account, relative to this darknefs, is, that " on the 8th of March, an hour before " fun-fet, the air, in the fuburb of Pidara, and fome " other neighbouring places, became fomewhat thick " and dark, with a darknefs fimilar to that which is " caufed by fome partial eclipfes of the fun."

The two other paffages, which I omit for the fake of brevity, are equally perverted.

Mr. Brydone, indeed, through his whole journey to Etna has fufficiently fhewn his attachment to the marvellous, and, where that has failed him, has had recourfe to the aid of his playful fancy to furnifh him with extravagant, though ingenious, inventions of the ridiculous kind. The ftory of the veil of St. Agatha is an example; which veil, according to him, the people of Catania confider as an infallible remedy againft volcanos, but which at the time of a great eruption " feemed to have loft its virtue; the torrent burfting " over the walls, and fweeping away the image of " every faint that was placed there to oppofe it." But

would

Phyſician of Naples cauſed to be taken on the ſpot, at the time, and which in the moſt natural manner repreſents this river of fire ſuch as it appeared at its beginning, during its progreſs, and at its end; it will likewiſe render much more intelligible ſeveral particulars of which I propoſe hereafter to treat. (See Plate I.)

Having mentioned theſe travellers, I ſhall make ſome obſervations on what has been ſaid by Count Borch relative to the changes that have taken place in the lava of 1669, would it not have been more commendable to have furniſhed his readers with real information, inſtead of filling ſo many pages with theſe trivial and inſipid pleaſantries? In fact, after having read his five letters on Etna, what idea do they enable us to form of the nature of this mountain?

I do not mean, by what I have ſaid, indiſcriminately to condemn the whole work of Mr. Brydone. His Tour frequently contains facts and obſervations well deſerving attention. It is elegantly written, and the author was well acquainted with the ſecret of exciting our curioſity, and rendering his narrative intereſting; though frequently, with that kind of intereſt which ſeems more ſuitable to romance than to authentic hiſtory.

and

and those of some other eruptions preceding, and posterior to, that time. These changes consist in the vegetable earth which begins to appear on them, generated in part from the decomposition of the lava, and in part from the destruction of the plants, which, after a certain time, are produced upon it. From the quantity of this earth he deduces a rule to judge of the age of the lava; which he endeavours to prove by examples of different Etnean lavas, of various epochs, which are covered with more or less of this earth in proportion as they are more or less ancient. Thus, a lava produced by an eruption in 1157, when he examined it in December 1776, had a coating of earth twelve inches thick; another which had flowed in 1329, had one of eight inches; on that of 1669, was found more than one inch; while the most recent, that of 1766, was entirely destitute of such earth. Whence he concludes, that, from the antiquity of the lavas, ascertained by the quantity of earth with which they are covered, may be deduced the antiquity of the world.

As

As this argument is certainly somewhat specious, and has been employed by others, it merits to be discussed. We undoubtedly know from repeated observations, that lavas, after a series of years, are invested with a stratum of earth proper for vegetation; and the fact has already been proved in this work: nor can it be denied that this earth is originally produced by the decomposition of the lavas, and that of the plants which have taken root upon it. The same may be observed in mountains not volcanized, the stones of which (at least very frequently), being long exposed to the action of the air and seasons, are resolved into an earth proper for the growth of vegetables. It would not, therefore, admit of a doubt that the more ancient lavas must afford a greater quantity of earth than those of more recent date, were every exterior circumstance equal; were they all of the same consistence and qualities, and all equally affected by the fire. But how greatly they differ in these respects we have already seen, and shall see still more in the progress of this work. Such differences, therefore,

therefore, muſt render the argument of Count Borch extremely inconcluſive; ſince a lava of an earlier age may have much leſs earth than one of later date; a circumſtance which the Chevalier Gioeni told me he had frequently obſerved in ſeveral of the lavas of Etna.

Among the lavas adduced by Count Borch, in favour of his hypotheſis, is that which flowed in 1329, which, when he examined it, that is four hundred and forty-ſeven years after its eruption, was covered with eight inches of earth. Yet the lava of the Arſo, in Iſchia, which ruſhed into the ſea in 1302, when I ſaw it in 1788, ſtill preſerved in every part its hardneſs and ſterility *.

It appears, likewiſe, extraordinary, that this writer ſhould not have noticed the remains of another current of lava near Catania, which has been employed for two thouſand years as materials for buildings, and which retains ſuch hardneſs, that where the labour of

* Chap. V.

the cultivator has not been exerted it still continues entirely sterile.

With respect to the lava of 1669, I cannot conceive how the Count could attribute to it an inch or more of earth, since it is entirely destitute of it. Were this the fact, the surface of the lava must at least, in some few places, exhibit some blades of grass, or small plants, as a stratum of earth an inch thick would be sufficient to nourish them; but we find it, on the contrary, destitute of every vegetable, except a few lichens, which we know will take root and grow on the hardest bodies, and such as entirely resist all effect of the air, as quartzes, and even on the smooth and slippery surface of vitreous substances. The Count, very possibly, examined this lava in low hollow places, into which the rainwater had drained, and brought down with it some particles of earth, that might have formed a thin stratum *.

* With respect to the uncertainty and fallacy of any calculations deduced from the greater or less quantity of vegetable earth which may cover lavas, the reader may consult the work of M. Dolomieu above cited.

Before

Before I travelled into Sicily, I had read the eulogiums bestowed on the Prince of Biscaris, by Count Borch, among other reasons, because he had exerted himself in attempts to change the face of the lava of 1669, and transform the ungrateful soil into a fruitful garden. When I arrived in the island, I admired the effect of human art. In many places the hardest lava had been opened by the force of mines; while in others it had been broken into extremely minute fragments, into which, when collected in certain receptacles, several kinds of useful plants had been inserted: but, unfortunately, they always perished, though they were repeatedly planted. Some few I found living, as here and there a pomegranate or an almond tree; but these were extremely weak and languid, though the broken lava among which they had taken root was mixed with vegetable earth. A species of the Indian fig*, alone, throve and flourished; but it is well known that this shrub delights in lavas, and

---

* Cactus opuntia. Linn.

that it will take root, grow to a confiderable height, and bear fruit plentifully, on the moſt ſterile. In the courſe of this work I ſhall have occaſion to treat more at length on this ſubject. At preſent there only remains a large pond which has been dug in the lava of a conſiderable depth, and communicating with the water of the ſea, in which are preſerved different kinds of fiſh.

After having, for a conſiderable time, examined the environs of Catania, aſſiſted by the Chevalier Gioeni, to whom I owe the moſt lively and ſincere gratitude for numerous favours; I ſet out for Mount Etna, on the morning of the 3d of September, accompanied, among others, by Carmelo Puglieſi, and Domenico Mazzagaglia, two guides extremely well acquainted with the roads. I performed the greater part of the journey on foot, only riding when I found myſelf fatigued. I think it ſcarcely neceſſary to mention, what has been ſo often repeated by travellers, and therefore muſt be ſo well known, that the lower region of Mount Etna, which extends
through

through twelve miles of the afcent towards the fummit, is incredibly abundant in paftures and fruit trees of every kind *.

It is alfo well known that this fertility is to be afcribed to the lava, which, foftened by length of time, has produced a moft fertile foil, thus compenfating paft calamity by prefent fruitfulnefs. To this, however, the induftry of man and arts of agriculture have not a little contributed; as well as the corruption and decompofition of vegetables, which have fo great a fhare in the fructification of the earth. Thefe lavas, however, in fome places, ftill manifeft their native

---

* The fertility of this region has been celebrated by the greater part of thofe authors who have written concerning Etna; among which the moft diftinguifhed are Strabo, and Fazello, but above all Peter Bembo, who, after having vifited the mountain, compofed an ingenious dialogue on the fubject. It may excite fome furprife, that, after fo many defcriptions of this region, and after Borelli, above a century before, had thought fuch a defcription fuperfluous; Mr. Brydone fhould imagine it worth while once more to recount the prodigies of this fertile foil.

wildnefs, rifing above the ufeful foil, in craggy points and tumours, or difcovering their naked fides on the banks of rapid torrents. On fome declivities, where the earth has but little depth, we find trees, the roots of which, not having been able to penetrate the unyielding lava, have turned afide, and extended horizontally along the furface of the foil. Whence it evidently appears that the fertility of the inferior region depends entirely on a cruft of earth, more or lefs thick, without which the fame barrennefs muft take place, which, it cannot be doubted, once prevailed.

At ten in the morning, I arrived at the village of Nicolofi, (Plate I. H.) near Monte Roffo, which formerly was a plain, when in 1669 a new vortex opened, and difgorged a dreadful torrent of lava, which poured headlong down until it reached the fea, where it formed a kind of promontory (Y). It would have been a great omiffion not to have vifited this mountain, though it lies a little out of the

the direct road up Etna. Besides the memorable eruption which has been mentioned more than once, other objects relative to it, which I had here an opportunity of examining on the spot, attracted my attention. Among these, was that quantity of black sand which was thrown out in that eruption from the new volcanic mouth, which still remains, and covers an extensive plain beyond Nicolosi, where once verdant trees flourished; some of which still preserve remains of life, and raise their leafy branches above the changing sand. This sand, which covers a circuit of two miles round Monte Rosso, when it was first ejected from the vortex, extended over a space of fifteen miles; and covered the ground to such a height, that the vines and shrubs were entirely buried. Some of the finer particles of it were carried by the southerly wind even to Calabria, where they fell thick in many places, as we are informed by Borelli.

As I approached the mountain, I found the depth of the sand greater, and it became a confiderable impediment in my way, as my leg frequently fank into it up to the knee. It is well known that this mountain is forked, being fo formed by the eruption, at which time it was called by the country people, Monte della Ruina (the Mountain of Ruin), and afterwards Monte Roffo (the Red Mountain), probably becaufe fome parts of it appeared of that colour. Borelli tells us, that its circumference at the bafe does not exceed two miles, and that its perpendicular height is not more than one hundred and fifty paces; while Sir William Hamilton eftimates its height at a mile, and its circuit at leaft at three. From the obfervations I have been able to make, I muft prefer the eftimate of the Italian mathematician to that of Sir William.

The accurate accounts of the fame Borelli inform us, that the gulf whence this eruption iffued opened on the 11th of March, 1669, about the time of the fetting of the fun; that the lava burft forth that fame night; and that, on the 13th of the fame month, a
fhower

shower of scoriæ and sand began to be cast into the air, which continued three months, and formed Monte Rosso. From among a hundred or more mountains which rear their heads on the sides of Mount Etna, this is the only one with the history of the formation of which we are acquainted *.

On examining this bifurcated mountain at the top, on the sides, and at the bottom, especially in those places where the rain-waters had produced furrows and deep excavations, I found it composed of different scoriæ and sand, that is to say, lava that had undergone various modifications, and from

* Sir William Hamilton, in his journey to Etna, speaking of this eruption, cites an account of it by the Earl of Winchelsea, who was present at the time, but which is more marvellous than true. He did not approach the place, but only beheld the eruption from the towers of Catania. He tells us, that the fire divided one mountain into two; and that it was composed, as were the stones and ashes vomited out (besides other principles), of mercury, lead, bronze, and every other kind of metal; which alone would be sufficient to deprive this account of all credit.

that same lava which has formed the immense current; as sufficiently appears from the identity of their principles. The base of this lava is the horn-stone: it is of a grey colour, dry in its fractures, rough to the touch, of a grain moderately fine, gives sparks with steel, and sounds when struck. It serves as a matrix to a great number of felt-spathose and shoerlaceous crystallizations *. If from this lava we turn our eyes to the scoriæ, of which Monte Rosso is principally composed, we observe the same kind of base, containing, in like manner, shoerls and feltspars; except only that the scoriæ have more lightness and friability, from their greater number of pores, which gives them the resemblance of certain spunges; besides that they have a kind of vitreous appearance, and that the pieces on

* I have given a brief description of this lava, as, in the present case, it seemed necessary; but, in future, I do not propose to describe the lavas and other productions of Etna; both because a month would not have been sufficient to have made a proper examination of them all, much less the short time I was able to employ in this journey; and because M. Dolomieu has already undertaken to give this description.

the furface are fcabrous; differences which arife from the fcoriæ having been more changed than the lavas by the activity of the fire, and that of the elaftic gafes.

When the volcano threw up a deluge of fcoriæ, a great number of them muft clafh, be broken, and reduced to powder; thus producing fhowers of fand: whence the fand that covers the environs of Monte Roffo, which, from the examinations I have made, I find to confift only of triturated fcoriæ. The lava of Monte Roffo, the fcoriæ, and the fand confift, therefore, of the fame component parts.

M. Dolomieu having found, at Monte Roffo, great numbers of detached fhoerls, of the fame kind with thofe which enter into the lava of that current; that is to fay, black, lamellated, flat, of a hexaedrous prifmatic form, and, for the moft part, terminated by a dihedrous pyramid, he thought, with apparent reafon, that they at firft entered into the body of the lava; he therefore

fore endeavoured to explain in what manner they were separated from it; having recourse to the sulphur, which, according to him, had scorified the lava, but had not been able to produce the same effect on the shoerls, from the small quantity of iron they contain, which, consequently, remained free and detached.

It is incredible how great a number of these loose shoerls are to be met with about Monte Rosso, and particularly on its top. When I was there, the sun shining clear, I saw them, in several places, sparkling on the ground, and I had only slightly to move the scoriæ and sand, to bring them to light by hundreds. They were exactly such as they are described by the French naturalist. I formed a design to ascertain the truth of the theory by which he has endeavoured to explain the separation of the shoerls from the lava, and when I returned to Pavia I made several experiments for that purpose. As his hypothesis was, that it proceeded from the shoerls containing a less quantity of iron than

than the lava, it was to be expected that the magnetic needle would be lefs affected by the former than the latter. From the experiments I made both with the lava, or, more properly fpeaking, its bafe, and with the detached fhoerls, I perceived that the needle was attracted by the former at the diftance of $\frac{1}{4}$, $\frac{1}{3}$, and even $\frac{1}{2}$ a line, while the attractive force of the detached fhoerls acted on it at the diftance of $\frac{1}{4}$ of a line, $\frac{1}{3}$ of a line, and a whole line; one fhoerl even gave manifeft figns of attraction at the diftance of a line and a half. It is fcarcely neceffary to remark, that in fuch experiments every acceffary circumftance ought to be equal; that is, the pieces of lava ought to be equal in fize, and of the fame configuration with the detached fhoerls. Thefe experiments prevented my adopting the theory in queftion, fince they fhewed that the martial principle was much more abundant in the fhoerls than in their bafe; contrary to the hypothefis of M. Dolomieu. Reflecting, however, on the phenomenon of the ifolated fhoerls, another mode of explanation occurred to me, which

which I shall here submit to the judgment of the learned reader.

Experience has shewn, that the volcanic fire which melted the lava was incapable of melting the shoerls, as they are found within it as completely crystallized, with angles as acute, and of the same lustre, as those which are detached among the sand and scoriæ. As they are therefore so refractory to the fire, and are, besides, of a different specific gravity from the lava, it may reasonably be supposed that, when the latter was melted, and, in the eruption of 1669, forced by elastic vapours to a prodigious height, where it was separated into small particles, numbers of shoerls were detached from it, and fell, isolated, partly within the crater, and partly around it. As these showers of fiery lava continued three months, the number of shoerls which thus fell detached must have been very considerable, as we, in fact, find them at present.

The results produced by the furnace on these

these shoerls when detached are very different from those they exhibit when incorporated with the lava. In the former case they are infusible, though they should remain there several days. When minutely triturated, indeed, their particles will conglutinate together, but without forming a compact and vitreous body. The fusion, on the contrary, is perfect in those which are enveloped in the body of the lava. Monte Rosso, quite to the sea, abounds in such shoerls. A few hours in the furnace are sufficient to change them into a shining, compact, and extremely hard enamel. Some lineament of the feltspars contained in the lava always remains; but it is impossible to discover any traces of the shoerls, they having formed, with their base, which has passed into the state of enamel, a similar and homogeneous body. The base of this lava, which, as we have said, is of hornstone, has therefore acted as a flux on the shoerls.

This experiment throws light on another subject

subject of some importance, already mentioned in Chap. V. which treats of Ischia; where speaking of the fusion obtained in the furnace of some feltspars, though detached, of some of the lavas of that island, I observed that it is not always true that the feltspars are more difficult to fuse than shoerls, as is generally imagined. I then alluded to what is here detailed, though this is not the only place where that truth will be proved.

I shall make another remark or two on these shoerls. They do not belong, exclusively, to this lava of Monte Rosso, but are found in many others of Mount Etna.

I do not know that any attempt has been hitherto made to analyse them chemically. I therefore undertook to ascertain their component principles by the process with asbestine earth invented by Bergman. From 100 docimastic pounds of these shoerls I obtained the following result:

Silex

	Pounds.
Silex	34,5
Lime	18,7
Iron	7,6
Alum	12,4
Magnesia	11,
	Sum 84,2 *

Monte Roffo (the Red Mountain), as we have already faid, has received this name from fome parts of it being tinged with that colour, though there are others which are white, and others yellow. All thefe parts of it are found to be more or lefs decompofed, and, in general, they are only fcoriæ. It feems indubitable that thefe colours are produced by iron, changed or modified by acids.

Some of thefe fcoriæ, which have not been

---

* It muft be remarked, that befides the almoft irreparable lofs in manipulation, and that of the water pre-exifting in the fhoerls, the lime is here deprived of the acid with which it was before combined.

affected

affected by the action of the acids, exhibit a remarkable phenomenon. They are covered with a thin coat of pellucid glafs, and feem as if a fheet of water had flowed over them and been fuddenly frozen. This appearance, which in the neighbourhood of any other volcano would not merit a moment's regard, is remarkable at Etna, becaufe we there meet with no vitrifications; M. Dolomieu, whofe induftry and accuracy are fo great in all his refearches, having found only one piece, and that of uncertain origin.

This vitreous integument has very probably been occafioned by a more energetic action of the fire.

After I had ftaid fome time at Monte Roffo, equally to my inftruction and amufement; and had viewed with admiration the trunk and branches of that extenfive river of lava, which iffuing from the root of the mountain, and inundating an immenfe tract of country, had rufhed into the fea; I took my way towards the monaftery of St. Niccolo
dell'

dell' Arena, a pleasing resting-place for travellers who visit Etna, where I arrived about noon on the 3d of September. This very ancient edifice, founded on the lava, was the habitation of a number of Benedictine monks, who about two hundred years ago, in consequence of the devastation occasioned by the lava, were obliged to abandon it, and retire to Catania. The injuries it has at different times suffered are recorded in various inscriptions still remaining, which commemorate ruinous earthquakes, torrents of lava, and showers of sand and ashes, by which it has been damaged and almost destroyed; with the dates of the different repairs. The environs of this place would still be entirely covered with the black sand thrown up by Monte Rosso in 1669, were it not that this sand becomes more easily changed into vegetable earth than the lava; and, for many years, has been planted with more than one extensive vineyard. After taking a slight refreshment in this hospitable place, I continued my journey towards the summit of Etna, proceeding over ancient lavas, which

which were still every where unproductive of any kind of vegetable.

About three miles above San Niccolo dell' Arena, the lower region of Etna ends, and the middle begins, which extends for ten miles, or nearly that distance, in a direct line, up the mountain. It is, with great propriety, called *selvosa*, or the woody region; since it abounds with aged oaks, beeches, firs, and pines. The soil of this region is a vegetable earth, generated by the decomposition of the lavas, and similar to that in the lower region; which lavas may not only every where be found on digging a little depth into the ground, but display themselves uncovered in many places, as we have already remarked of the lavas of the other region. The middle region is celebrated for its luxuriant vegetation and its lofty trees; but it appeared to me scarcely to deserve this celebrity. The trees (at least in the places where I noticed them), and especially the oaks, which form the greatest part of this woody zone, are low, and as I may say stinted in their growth;

and

and would lose much when compared with those of other countries. The beeches, which grow only on the upper extremity of the zone, would appear mere pigmies, if placed beside those which rear their lofty heads on the Apennines and the Alps. This, I am of opinion, is to be attributed to the little depth of the earth proper for vegetation. The woods and verdure of these two regions, the inferior and the middle, are recorded by the greater part of the writers of antiquity; so that the commencement of this vegetation appears to be lost in the obscurity of time. How much more ancient, then, must have been the date of the flowing of those lavas to the slow decomposition of which the vegetation owes its origin!

Before the day closed, I reached the celebrated Grotta delle Capre, but it only afforded us a wretched couch of leaves and straw. It is, however, the only place where the traveller can rest who wishes early in the morning to reach the top of Etna, which is eight miles diftant. It is one of thofe caverns which we frequently meet with in the middle of the lavas of that immenfe mountain; and a little higher begins the laft and fublime region. Here I ftopped to pafs the night; but, before I endeavoured to compofe myfelf to fleep, I found it very agreeable to warm myfelf by a fire made with fome branches cut from the neighbouring trees; as, at this height, Reaumur's thermometer ftood at $8\frac{1}{2}$ degrees above the freezing point (51° of Fahrenheit); while in the morning of the fame day, at Catania, it had been at 23° (72 of Fahrenheit). Cafting my eye around the grotto, I perceived the names of feveral travellers; fome of them names of eminence, with the dates when they had been here, cut on the trunks of feveral of the oaks; but I muft confefs that I felt fome little indignation on remarking that among all thefe there was not one Italian name.

I fhall conclude this chapter with fome remarks relative to an object that has not, to my knowledge, been attended to by any other traveller. We have been told that the grotto is called La Grotta delle Capre (the grotto of the goats) becaufe goats are ufed to be fhut in it, in rainy weather; that it is hollowed in the lava in the fhape of a furnace; that it is furrounded with ancient and venerable oaks; that leaves, there, compofe the beds of travellers; but no one has yet defcribed the qualities of the lava of which it is formed. Without pretending perfectly to fupply this omiffion, I fhall fay that the lava here is of a horn-ftone bafe; that it is of an earthy texture; and that, though it abounds with pores and vacuities, it has confiderable hardnefs. It contains fome fhoerls, and likewife two kinds of feltfpars; fome of a flat figure, which are extremely brilliant in the fractures; the others of an irregular fhape, with little luftre, and which manifeft a degree of calcination, though without any indication of fufion. A few other thin fmall ftones are interfperfed in them, which from their hardnefs and green colour I incline to think are chryfolites;

lites; as it is known that thefe noble ftones are found in many of the lavas of Etna.

This lava in the furnace is transformed into an enamel full of bubbles; and as it then changes to a blacker colour, the white feltfpars become more confpicuous. The magnetic needle is acted upon by it at the diftance of a line and a half. The other lavas of the vicinity do not differ from that of the Grotta delle Capre, or rather they are a continuation of the fame, even where they are covered by a ftratum of earth and a multitude of trees. It is therefore evident, that this grotto has been formed from time immemorial; and that it is not the work of the rain-water, but has been produced by the action of the elaftic gafes of the lavas when they were fluid, which have generated in them this hollow place, as they have, elfewhere, many others, of which we may have occafion hereafter to treat.

CHAP.

CHAP. VIII.

CONTINUATION OF THE JOURNEY TO ETNA.

Upper region of Etna—Destitute of vegetables—Its lavas—View of the rising sun from those heights—Lavas which issued from the principal crater of Etna in the months of July and October 1787—Difficulty of crossing those lavas to arrive at the summit of Etna—After burning eleven months and more, some places not yet extinguished—Other difficulties—Arrival at the top of Etna—Clear view of the great crater, circumference of the great crater, with other particulars—Etna a bifurcated mountain—Another smaller crater—Obstacles usually met with in a journey to Mount Etna—Comparison of what the author observed within the crater of Mount Etna, with the observations before made by M. Riedesel, Sir William Hamilton, Brydone, and Borch—

Borch—*Physical causes of the changes in volcanic craters*—*Ancient accounts of these changes*—*Large masses have sometimes fallen from the top of Etna into the crater*—*No sensible diminution of the height of this mountain in the times of which we have any account*—*Various phenomena observable in the smoke which at different times has exhaled from the Etnean furnace*—*No inconvenience experienced by the author from the thinness of the air on the top of Etna*—*The effect of this different, on different individuals*—*Extensive and admirable prospect from the summit of Etna.*

THREE hours before day, I, with my companions, left the Grotta delle Capre, which had afforded us a welcome asylum, though our bed was not of the softest, as it consisted only of a few oak leaves scattered over the floor of lava. I continued my journey towards the summit of Etna; and the clearness of the sky induced me to hope that it would continue the same during the approaching day, that I might enjoy the extensive tenfive and fublime profpect from the top of this lofty mountain, which is ufually involved in clouds. I foon left the middle region, and entered the upper one, which is entirely deftitute of vegetation, except a few bufhes very thinly fcattered. The light of feveral torches which were carried before us enabled me to obferve the nature of the ground over which we paffed, and to afcertain, from fuch experiments as I was able to make, that our road lay over lavas either perfectly the fame with, or analogous to, thofe in which the Grotta delle Capre is hollowed.

We had arrived at within about four miles of the borders of the great crater, when the dawn of day began to difperfe the darknefs of night. Faint gleams of a whitifh light were fucceeded by the ruddy hues of aurora; and foon after the fun rofe above the horizon, turbid at firft and dimmed by mifts, but his rays infenfibly became more clear and refplendent. Thefe gradations of the rifing day are no where to be viewed with fuch precifion and delight, as from the lofty
height

height we had reached, which was not far from the moſt elevated point of Etna. Here, likewiſe, I began to perceive the effects of the eruption of Etna which took place in July 1787, and which has been ſo accurately deſcribed by the Chevalier Gioeni*. Theſe were viſible in a coating of black ſcoriæ, at firſt thin, but which became gradually thicker as I approached the ſummit of the mountain, till it compoſed a ſtratum of ſeveral palms in thickneſs. Over theſe ſcoriæ I was obliged to proceed, not without confiderable difficulty and fatigue, as my leg at every ſtep ſank deep into it. The figure of theſe ſcoriæ, the ſmalleſt of which are about a line or ſomewhat leſs in diameter, is very irregular. Externally they have the appearance of ſcoriæ of iron; and, when broken, are found full of ſmall cavities, which are almoſt all ſpherical, or nearly of that figure. They are, therefore, light and friable; two qualities which are almoſt always inſeparable from

---

* His account of this eruption was printed at Catania in 1787. There is likewiſe a French tranſlation at the end of the *Catalogue Raiſonné* of M. Dolomieu.

scoriæ. This great number of cavities is an evident proof of the quantity and vigorous action of the elastic fluids, which in this eruption, imprisoned in the liquid matter within the crater, dilated it on every side, seeking to extricate themselves; and forced it, in scoriaceous particles, to various heights and distances, according to the respective weights of those particles. The most attentive eye cannot discover in them the smallest shoerl; either because these stones have been perfectly fused, and with the lava passed into one homogeneous consistence; or because they never existed in it. Some linear felspars are however found, which by their splendour, semi-transparency, and solidity, shew that they have suffered no injury from the fire. When these scoriæ are pulverized, they become extremely black; but retain the drynefs and scabrous contexture which they had when entire. They abound in iron, and in consequence the dust produced by pulverizing them copiously adheres to the point of a magnetized knife; and a small piece of these scoriæ will put

the

the magnetic needle in motion at the diftance of two lines.

In the midft of this immenfe quantity of fcoriæ, I, in feveral places, met with fome fubftances of a fpherical figure, which, like the lava, were at firft fmall, but increafed in fize as I approached the fummit of the mountain. Thefe were originally particles of lava ejected from the crater in the eruption before mentioned, which affumed a fpherical figure when they were congealed by the coldnefs of the air. On examining them, I found them in their qualities perfectly to refemble the fcoriæ, and to poffefs the fame magnetifm.

Only two miles and a half remained of our journey, when the great laboratory of nature, inclofed within the abyffes of Etna, began its aftonifhing operations. Two white columns of fmoke arofe from its fummit; one, which was the fmalleft, towards the north-eaft fide of the mountain; and the other, towards the north-weft. A light wind blowing

blowing from the eaſt, they both made a curve towards the weſt, gradually dilating, until they diſappeared in the wide expanſe of air. Several ſtreams of ſmoke, which aroſe lower down, towards the weſt, followed the two columns. Theſe appearances could not but tend to inſpire me with new ardour to proſecute my journey, that I might diſcover and admire the ſecrets of this ſtupendous volcano. The ſun, likewiſe, ſhining in all his ſplendour, ſeemed to promiſe that this day ſhould crown my wiſhes. But experience taught me that the two miles and a half I had yet to go preſented many more obſtacles than I could have imagined, and that nothing but the reſolution I had formed to complete my deſign at every hazard could have enabled me to ſurmount them.

Having proceeded about a hundred paces further, I met with a torrent of lava, which I was obliged to croſs, to arrive at the ſmoking ſummit. My guides informed me that this lava had iſſued from the mountain in October 1787; and as the account of the

Chevalier

Chevalier Gioeni, which I have above cited, only mentions the eruption of the month of July of the same year, I shall here give a brief description of it; as it does not seem hitherto to have been described.

This very recent lava extends three miles in length; its breadth is various, in some places being about a quarter of a mile, in others one third, and in others still more. Its height, or rather depth, is different in different parts; the greatest being, as far as I was able to observe, about eighteen feet, and the least six. Its course is down the west side of the mountain; and, like the other lava which flowed in the July of 1787, it issued immediately from the great crater of Etna. The whole number of the eruptions of this mountain of which we have any record, before and after the Christian era, is thirty-one; and ten only, as we are informed by Gioeni, including that of which he has given an account, have issued immediately from the highest crater. That which I observed may be the eleventh, unless it should rather be
considered

considered as the same with that described by the Sicilian naturalist; since the interval between August and October is a very short intermission of rest for a volcano. The cause of the rarity of the eruptions which issue immediately from the crater, compared with those which disgorge from the sides, seems easily to be assigned. The centre of this volcano is probably at a great depth, and perhaps on a level with the sea. It is, therefore, much more easy for the matter liquefied by the fire, put in effervescence by the elastic fluids, and impelled on every side from the centre to the circumference, to force its way through one of the sides of the mountain where it finds least resistance, and there form a current, than to be thrown up, notwithstanding the resistance of gravity, from the bottom to so great a height as the highest crater of Etna. It is evident, therefore, that the effervescence in the eruptions of the months of July and October 1787 was extremely violent. The torrent of the month of October is every where covered with scoriæ, which resemble those ejected in the month of July in their black colour,

lour, but differ from them in the great adhesion they have to the lava, in their exterior vitreous appearance, their greater weight, and their hardness, which is so great that they give sparks with steel almost as plentifully as flints. These differences, however, are to be attributed only to accidental combinations of the same substance; the constituent principles of the scoriæ of this lava not being different from those of the detached scoriæ mentioned above. Both, likewise, contain the same felspar lamellæ.

This new current was, however, extremely difficult, and even dangerous, in the passage. In some places the scoriæ projected in prominent angles and points, and in others sunk in hollows, or steep declivities; in some, from their fragility and smoothness, they resembled thin plates of ice, and in others they presented vertical and sharp projections. In addition to these difficulties, my guides informed me I should have to pass three places where the lava was still red-hot, though it was now eleven months since

since it had ceased to flow. These obstacles, however, could not overcome my resolution to surmount them, and I then experienced, as I have frequently done at other times, how much may be effected, in difficulties and dangers like these, by mere physical courage, by the assistance of which we may proceed along the edge of a precipice in safety; while the adventurer who suffers himself to be surprised by a panic fear will be induced cowardly to desist from the enterprise he might have completed. In several places, it is true, the scoriæ broke under my feet; and in others I slipped, and had nearly fallen into cavities from which I should have been with difficulty extricated. One of the three places pointed out by the guides had, likewise, from its extreme heat, proved highly disagreeable; yet, at length, I surmounted all these obstacles and reached the opposite side, not without making several cursory observations on the places whence those heats originated. Two large clefts, or apertures, in different places appeared in the lava, which there, notwithstanding the clearness of the day, had an obscure redness: and on applying the end of the staff which I used as a support in this difficult journey, to one of these, it presently smoked, and, immediately after, took fire. It was, therefore, indubitable that this heap of ejected lava still contained within it the active remains of fire, which were more manifest there, than in other places, because those matters were there collected in greater quantities.

I had yet to encounter other obstacles. I had to pass that tract which may properly be called the cone of Etna, and which, in a right line, is about a mile, or somewhat more, in length. This was extremely steep, and not less rugged, from the accumulated scoriæ which had been heaped upon it in the last eruption, the pieces of which were neither connected together, nor attached to the ground; so that, frequently, when I stepped upon one of them, before I could advance my other foot, it gave way, and, forcing other pieces before it down the steep declivity,

clivity, carried me with it, compelling me to make many steps backwards instead of one forwards. To add to this inconvenience, the larger pieces of scoriæ above that on which I had stepped, being deprived of the support of those contiguous to them, came rolling down upon me, not without danger of violently bruising my feet, or breaking my legs. After several ineffectual attempts to proceed, I found the only method to avoid this inconvenience, and continue my journey, was to step only on those larger pieces of scoriæ which, on account of their weight, remained firm: but the length of the way was thus more than doubled, by the circuitous windings it was necessary to make to find such pieces of scoriæ as from their large size were capable of affording a stable support. I employed three hours in passing, or rather dragging myself, to the top of the mountain, partly from being unable to proceed in a right line, and partly from the steepness of the declivity, which obliged me to climb with my hands and feet, sweating and breathless, and under the necessity of stopping at intervals to rest, and recover my strength. How much did I then envy the good fortune of those who had visited Etna before the eruption of 1787, when, as my guides assured me, the journey was far less difficult and laborious!

I was not more than a hundred and fifty paces distant from the vertex of the cone, and already beheld close to me, in all their majesty, the two columns of smoke. Anxious to reach the borders of the stupendous gulf, I summoned the little strength I had remaining, to make a last effort, when an unforeseen obstacle, for a moment, cruelly retarded the completion of my ardent wishes. The volcanic craters, which are still burning more or less, are usually surrounded with hot sulphureous acid steams, which issue from their sides, and rise in the air. From these the summit of Etna is not exempt; but the largest of them rose to the west, and I was on the south-east side. Here, likewise, four or five streams of smoke arose, from a part somewhat lower; and through these it was necessary to pass; since

on

on one fide was a dreadful precipice, and on the other fo fteep a declivity that I and my companion, from weaknefs and fatigue, were unable to afcend it; and it was with the utmoft difficulty that our two guides made their way up it, notwithftanding they were fo much accuftomed to fuch laborious expeditions. We continued our journey, therefore, through the midft of the vapours; but though we ran as faft as the ground and our ftrength would permit, the fulphureous fteams with which they were loaded were extremely offenfive, and prejudicial to refpiration; and affected me, in particular, fo much, that for fome moments I was deprived of fenfe; and found, by experience, how dangerous an undertaking it is to vifit volcanic regions infefted by fuch vapours.

Having paffed this place, and recovered by degrees my former prefence of mind; in lefs than an hour I arrived at the utmoft fummit of Etna, and began to difcover the edges of the crater; when our guides, who had preceded me at fome diftance, turned back, and, haſtening towards me, exclaimed in a kind of tranſport, that I never could have arrived at a more proper time to diſcover and obſerve the internal part of this ſtupendous volcano. The reader will eaſily conceive, without my attempting to deſcribe it, how great a pleaſure I felt at finding my labours and fatigue at length crowned with ſuch complete ſucceſs. This pleaſure was exalted to a kind of rapture, when I had completely reached the ſpot, and perceived that I might, without danger, contemplate this amazing ſpectacle. I ſat down near the edge of the crater, and remained there two hours, to recover my ſtrength after the fatigues I had undergone in my journey. I viewed with aſtoniſhment the configuration of the borders, the internal ſides, the form of the immenſe cavern, its bottom, an aperture which appeared in it, the melted matter which boiled within, and the ſmoke which aſcended from it. The whole of this ſtupendous ſcene was diſtinctly diſplayed before me; and I ſhall now proceed to give ſome deſcription of it, though it will

will only be poffible to prefent the reader with a very feeble image, as the fight alone can enable him to form ideas at all adequate to objects fo grand and aftonifhing.

The upper edges of the crater, to judge by the eye, are about a mile and a half in circuit, and form an oval, the longeft diameter of which extends from eaft to weft. As they are in feveral places broken, and crumbled away in large fragments, they appear as it were indented, and thefe indentations are a kind of enormous fteps, formed of projecting lavas and fcoriæ. The internal fides of the cavern, or crater, are inclined in different angles in different places. To the weft their declivity is flight: they are more fteep to the north; ftill more fo to the eaft; and to the fouth-eaft, on which fide I was, they are almoft perpendicular. Notwithftanding this irregularity, however, they form a kind of funnel; large at the top, and narrow at the bottom; as we ufually obferve in other craters. The fides appear irregularly rugged, and abound with

concretions

concretions of an orange colour, which, at firſt, I took for ſulphur; but, afterwards, found to be the muriate of ammoniac; having been able to gather ſome pieces of it from the edges of the gulf. The bottom is nearly a horizontal plane, about two-thirds of a mile in circumference. It appears ſtriped with yellow, probably from the above-mentioned ſalt. In this plain, from the place where I ſtood, a circular aperture was viſible, apparently about five poles in diameter, from which iſſued the larger column of ſmoke, which I had ſeen before I arrived at the ſummit of Etna. I ſhall not mention ſeveral ſtreams of ſmoke, which aroſe like thin clouds from the ſame bottom, and different places in the ſides. The principal column, which at its origin might be about twenty feet in diameter, aſcended rapidly in a perpendicular direction, while it was within the crater; but, when it had riſen above the edges, inclined towards the weſt, from the action of a light wind; and, when it had riſen higher, dilated into an extended but thin volume. This ſmoke was white, and,

being

being impelled to the fide oppofite that on which I was, did not prevent my feeing within the aperture; in which, I can affirm, I very diftinctly perceived a liquid ignited matter, which continually undulated, boiled, and rofe and fell; without fpreading over the bottom. This certainly was the melted lava which had arifen to that aperture from the bottom of the Etnean gulf.

The favourable circumftance of having this aperture immediately under my view induced me to throw into it fome large ftones, by rolling them down the fteep declivity below me. Thefe ftones, which were only large pieces of lava that I had detached from the edges of the crater, bounding down the fide, in a few moments fell on the bottom, and thofe which entered into the aperture, and ftruck the liquid lava, produced a found fimilar to that they would have occafioned had they fallen into a thick tenacious pafte. Every ftone I thus threw ftruck againft and loofened others in its paffage, which fell with it, and in like manner

ner struck and detached others in their way, whence the sounds produced were considerably multiplied. The stones which fell on the bottom rebounded, even when they were very large, and returned a sound different from that I have before described. The bottom cannot, therefore, be considered as only a thin crust; since, were it not thick and solid, it must have been broken by stones so heavy falling from so great a height.

This description will, perhaps, be better understood by an inspection of Plate II, which exhibits the summit of Mount Etna surrounded with large pieces and masses of lava. A A A represents one edge of the lava of 1787, which issued from the upper crater. B B the circumference of the crater, with its cleft C C, through which the internal part is discernible. D the flat bottom of the crater. E the aperture in the bottom, from which the larger column of smoke F F arose; which aperture, though it was on one side of the bottom, is, for the greater perspicuity, represented in the middle.

G G

G G that part of the edge of the crater from which its internal part is moſt diſtinctly viſible; and where the deſign of it might moſt conveniently be taken. H H the ſmaller column of ſmoke to the north-eaſt.

To ſatisfy one emotion of curioſity, is frequently to excite another. I had, at firſt, approached this volcano with a kind of ſuperſtitious awe. The hiſtories of every age, the relations of travellers, the univerſal voice of Europe, had all contributed to inſpire thoſe who ſhould adventure to viſit it with dread: but as at this time it ſeemed to have laid aſide its terrors, and was in a ſtate of perfect calmneſs and tranquillity, I was encouraged to become more familiar, and to endeavour to pry into more of its ſecrets. I have already obſerved that the ſide of the crater to the weſt is of a more gentle declivity than the others; and I, therefore, conceived that this might ſerve me as a ladder to deſcend to the bottom; where I might have added to the obſervations I had already made, other novel and important facts. But the perſons whom I had brought

with

with me as guides would not confent that I fhould expofe myfelf to fuch danger. They could not, however, prevent me frommaking, at my eafe, the obfervations I have here publifhed, and walking leifurely about the fummit of the mountain, notwithftanding the dangerous confequences with which they threatened me; telling me that, fhould the wind change, the column of fmoke muft be turned towards us, and might deprive us of life by its peftilential fumes; that, befides, we were not certain that the lava at the bottom, which now appeared fo calm and ftill, would long remain in the fame ftate; but that it was poffible, from circumftances difficult to forefee, that it might be thrown up on a fudden, and punifh our imprudent curiofity by burying us beneath the fiery ruin; in fupport of which fuggeftion they produced feveral inftances of fudden and moft unexpected eruptions.

We have feen above, that there were two columns of fmoke arifing from Etna. It is to be remarked that, befides that point

of

of Mount Etna on which I stood, there is another to the north, a quarter of a mile higher, and which renders the summit of Etna properly bifurcated. Within the first prominence is sunk the crater I have described; and on the side of the other is the second, from which ascends a lesser column of smoke. The second crater is smaller by about the one half, than that I have already described; and the one is separated from the other only by a partition of scoriæ and accumulated lava, which lies in the direction of from east to west. I made my observations on this second crater from a small distance; but it was impossible to advance to it, on account of the numerous and thick streams of smoke by which it was surrounded. This, however, was no great disappointment, after having seen and examined the principal crater, which is that whence several currents of lava had issued in 1787. I ought, certainly, to consider myself as extremely fortunate, in being able to gratify my curiosity with so near and distinct a view of the objects I have described; as the guides assured me, that,
among

among all the times when they had conducted ſtrangers to the ſummit of Etna, this was the only one in which they had a clear and undiſturbed view of the internal parts of that immenſe gulf. After my return to Catania, the Chevalier Gioeni likewiſe declared to me that, in all his different excurſions to that mountain, he had never had a good fortune ſimilar to mine; and that, a month before my arrival, he had made a journey to Etna, with the Chevalier Dangios, furniſhed with the neceſſary inſtruments to aſcertain accurately the height of the mountain; but when they had arrived at the foot of the cone, where they had propoſed to begin their operations, they were obliged to return back from the obſtacles they met with, which, to ſay the truth, are commonly neither few nor ſmall.

Etna riſes to a prodigious height above the level of the ſea, and its ſummit is uſually covered with ſnows and ice, and obſcured with clouds, except when the latter are low and range along the ſides. The winds,

winds, likewise, frequently blow with such violence that persons can scarcely keep their feet, not to mention the acute cold which benumbs the limbs. But the most formidable impediments to the progress of the adventurers who attempt this perilous journey, are the streams of sulphureous vapour which rise on the sides, and the thick clouds of sulphureous smoke which burst forth from the mouth of the volcano, even when not in a state of agitation. It seems as if Nature had placed these noxious fumes as a guard to Etna, and other fiery mountains, to prevent the approach of curiosity, and secure her mysterious and wondrous labours from discovery. I should, however, justly incur the reproach of being ungrateful, were I not to acknowledge the generous partiality she appeared to manifest towards me. At the time I made my visit, the sky was clear, the mountain free from snows, the temperature of the atmosphere not incommodious, the thermometer standing at seven degrees above the freezing point (48° of Fahrenheit), and the wind favouring my design,

sign, by driving the smoke of the crater from me, which otherwise would alone have been sufficient to have frustrated all my attempts. The streams of smoke I met with in my way were, indeed, somewhat troublesome, but they might have been much more so; though, had our guides conducted us by another road, as, on my return to Catania, I found they might have done, we should have escaped this inconvenience.

It here will not be improper to compare these observations on the crater of Etna with those of Baron Riedesel, Sir William Hamilton, Mr. Brydone, and Count Borch; as such a comparison will shew the great changes which have taken place in this volcano, within the space of twenty years; that is, from the time when it was visited by Baron Riedesel, in 1767, to that of my journey, in 1788. At the time when that traveller made his observations, the crater was enlarged towards the east, with an aperture which now no longer exists. He has not given the measure of its circuit, nor has he he mentioned the interior aspect of the crater; probably because he had not seen it, having been, as I imagine, prevented by the quantity of smoke which, he tells us, continually ascended from it.

It is worthy of notice, however, that at that time there was not at the bottom of the crater the hard flat surface I have described; since the stones thrown into it did not return the smallest sound. Within the gulf itself, was heard a noise similar to that of the waves of the sea when agitated by a tempest, which noise, probably, proceeded from the lava within the bowels of the mountain, liquefied and in motion. We may hence conceive how easily a volcano may begin to rage on a sudden, though, before, apparently in a state of complete tranquillity; for if we suppose a superabundant quantity of elastic substances to have been suddenly developed in the liquid lava of Etna, either at the time when Baron Riedesel visited the crater, or when I observed it in a state of slight commotion within the gulf, it muſt immediately have ſwelled in every part, beating violently againſt the ſides of the caverns in which it was impriſoned, thundered among the deep cavities, and, burſting forth through the ſides, have poured out a river of fire; or, ſhould its violence have been there reſiſted, it would have ruſhed up within the crater, until it overflowed its brink, and deluged the ſides of the mountains with its torrents.

Sir William Hamilton, on the 26th of October 1769, arrived at the ſummit of Etna, with great difficulty, on account of the ſnows he met with in his way, the ſeverity of the atmoſphere, the ſulphureous vapours, and the violence of the wind. He was unable to view diſtinctly the lower parts of the crater, being prevented by the great quantity of ſmoke which iſſued from it; though, when this ſmoke was ſometimes driven away by the wind, he could diſcover that the crater was ſhaped like a funnel, diminiſhing until it ended in a point;

point; and that this funnel was incrusted over with salt and sulphur. The crater was two miles and a half in circumference.

From the time, therefore, of the journey of Baron Riedesel to that of Sir William Hamilton, the crater must have undergone great changes in its structure; since, if the stones that were thrown into it gave no indications to the ear that they struck against any solid body, it is manifest that there must then have been an abyss as well as a funnel; and as the funnel terminated in a point, when it was observed by Sir William Hamilton, it is evident that the flat bottom I have described, and which was about two-thirds of a mile in circuit, did not then exist.

The internal sides of the crater, Sir William tells us, were covered with a crust of salt and sulphur: but he does not specify the nature of the former; and though the presence of the latter is not improbable, he might have been led into a mistake by the yellow colour, and have taken the muriate of ammoniac (sal ammoniac) for sulphur, as I did before I had examined it. Sir William has not told us that he made any examination at all; and it is probable that he judged only from the appearance it presented to his eye.

He observes, lastly, that the crater was two miles and a half in circumference; an estimate which may be made to agree with mine by neglecting the partition which separates the greater crater from the less, and considering them both as one. The sum of the two circumferences, according to the estimate I have given, would not then greatly differ from the measure of Sir William Hamilton. Nothing, likewise, can be more probable, than that among the various changes that have happened to Etna, this partition, by which the great crater is divided into two parts, has been produced.

Omitting the observations of Mr. Brydone,

done, that " the tremendous gulf of Etna, " fo'celebrated in all ages, has been looked " upon as the terror both of this and " another life ; that it infpires fuch awe " and horror, that it is not furprifing " that it has been confidered as the place " of the damned;" and other fimilar philofophical reflections which he has employed; and confining ourfelves to what he actually faw on the 29th of May 1770, we learn from him that " the crater was " then a circle of about three miles and a " half in circumference; that it went fhel- " ving down on each fide, and formed a " regular hollow, like a vaft amphitheatre; " and that a great mouth opened near the " centre*.

From the time of the journey of Sir William Hamilton, therefore, to that of the vifit of Brydone, that is to fay, within the fhort fpace of a year, various changes had happened to this volcano, by the enlarge-

* Brydone's Tour through Sicily and Malta, vol. i. p. 195, 196.

ment of its crater, and a spacious aperture formed in its bottom.

Count Borch appears to have wished to exceed the three other travellers in brevity, relative to this subject; since he only tells us that he arrived at the mountain on the 16th of December 1776, and that the crater of Etna is formed like a funnel. He adds, however, what is worthy of notice, that the summit of Etna is bifurcated, as I observed it to be: a circumstance not noticed by others, Sir William Hamilton even affirming that the summit of the mountain is single; whence we may conclude that one of these summits has been produced since the time of the journey of Brydone, in 1770.

On comparing the above-cited observations, made within the space of twenty-one years, we may perceive how many changes have taken place in Etna, during that interval; and, as, within that time, the mountain has suffered only two violent convulsions, fions, in the eruptions of 1781 and 1787, it is evident that, even in the ftate of apparent inaction, it ftill internally exerts its force.

To thefe obfervations it may, likewife, not be without utility to add thofe of M. D'Orville. He afcended Etna, in 1727, and remarked two craters; one larger than the other. The latter he only mentions, but the former he defcribes at fome length. Its circumference was, perhaps, fomewhat more than four miles. From it iffued clouds of fmoke and reddifh flames. Thefe, however, did not prevent his approaching to the edge of the gulf; though, to prevent the danger of falling into it, he and his companions faftened themfelves to a rope held by three men. On looking into the crater, they were unable to difcern the bottom, on account of the flames and fmoke: they only obferved that a conical hill, formed of lava, rofe in the middle of the crater, the top of which they eftimated to be fixty feet below them; and they were able to fee, perhaps, about sixty feet lower; where they conjectured the circuit of this hill might be from six hundred to eight hundred feet*.

We have here a remarkable circumstance relative to Etna, as it appeared in the time of M. D'Orville, and not observed by any one of the four travellers above cited—I mean the conical hill within the crater. Every observation, therefore, tends to confirm the inconstancy of the internal configuration and dimensions of this volcano. It is an extinguished forge, which, in proportion to the violence of the fire, to the nature of the fossil matters on which it acts, and of the elastic fluids which urge and set it in motion, produces, destroys, and re-produces various forms. The usual and natural figure of the summit of a volcanic mountain is that of an inverted concave cone, within, and one solid and erect without; and such a configuration, in countries which are no longer in a state of conflagration, is one of the most certain indications of the existence

* Jacobi Philippi D'Orville Sicula.

of an ancient volcano. This cone, however, is liable to very great changes; according to the greater or lefs fury of the volcano, and the quantity and quality of the matters ejected. Its internal part, from more than one caufe, is expofed to continual violence and change. The prodigious cavities of the mountain make it almoft appear fufpended in the air. It may eafily, therefore, give way, and fall in; efpecially on the violent impulfe of new matters which endeavour to force a paffage through the upper part; in confequence of which the inverted cone may, according to circumftances, prefent the appearance of an aperture, or whirlpool, or a gulf. Should the liquid lava pafs through the aperture, and continue there fome time, its fuperficies, by the contact of the cold air, lofing its heat gradually, would congeal, and form a cruft or folid plain; and fhould the fluid lava beneath, afterwards, act forcibly on this cruft, it might burft it, or make a paffage where it found leaft refiftance; in which cafe the melted lava would occupy that aperture. Should then the cruft, inftead of afcending in a fingle body, be be forced up in small fragments, these, cooled in the air, would fall down, in immense quantities, within the crater, and, from the effect of the laws of gravity, must accumulate in the figure of a cone. These theoretical conjectures, if they do not perfectly explain, may at least enable us to conceive, the nature of the causes which have produced the difference of appearance observed at different times in the crater of Etna.

It is much to be regretted that we have no history of Etna; which, did we possess it, must greatly contribute to elucidate the theory of volcanos, and the causes of the various changes which have taken place, at different times, in the summit of this mountain. That such changes have happened, is evident from the few, but valuable, notices concerning Etna, which we find in ancient authors. Of these I shall briefly state two or three which appear to be of most importance.

I shall first produce the authority of Strabo, though he was not himself an ocular witness, but relied on the information of others, who had visited Etna, and from whom he received the account, " That the " summit was a level plain, of about twenty " stadia in circumference, surrounded by a " brow, or ridge, of the height of a wall; " and that in the middle of the plain arose " a smoky hill, the smoke of which ascended " in a direct line, to the height of two hun- " dred feet*."

If we consider this description as accurate, the crater of Etna was at that time surrounded by a brow or ridge, which I should explain as the sides or edges; and, in the lower part, was separated by a mount rising in the middle †. The same geographer re-

* Οι δ'ουν νεωςὶ ἀναβαντες διηγανίο ἡμιν, οτι καταλαβοιεν ἀνω πεδιον ὁμαλον, ὁσον εικοσι ϛαδιων την περιμέιρον, κλειομενον ὀφρυι τεφρωδει, τειχικυ το ὑψος ἐχοιτι, ϛραντε το μεσον βουνον τεφρωδη την χροαν, ὑπερ δε του βουνου νεφος ὀρθιον διανεϛηκος εις ὑψος ὁσον διακοσιων ποδων εικαζειν δε καπνω.

† This observation agrees with that of D'Orville mentioned above. I find, likewise, that similar mounts have sometimes been thrown up within the crater of Vesuvius. De Bottis *Istoria di varj incendj del Vesuvio*.

lates

lates that two men, having ventured to descend upon that plain, were obliged immediately to return, from the violence of the heat*.

Solinus tells us that there were two craters from which the vapours issued†.

Cardinal Bembo likewise found two craters on the summit, the one higher than the other, and about as far distant as a stone might be thrown from a sling. The extreme violence of the wind, and the exhaling fumes, prevented him from approaching the upper crater. The lower he found to be formed like an immense pit, and surrounded with a plain of no great extent, which was so hot that he could not bear his hand on it. From its mouth, as from a chimney, continually issued a column of smoke.

* Δυο δε τολμησανlας προσελθειν εις το πεδιον· επεδε θερμοτερας εβαινον της αμμου και βαθυτερας, αναςρεψαι, μηδεν εχονlας περιllερον φραζειν των φαινομενων τοις πορρωθεν αφορωσι.

† In Etnæ vertice hiatus duo sunt, crateres nominati, per quos eructatus erumpit vapor. Cap. xi.

Of the other crater, which he could not obferve himfelf, hereceived a defcription, at Catania, from a monk, who, he affures us, was a man deferving credit, and well acquainted with fuch fubjects. He informed him that this crater was fituated on the higheft part of the fummit of Etna; that it was about three miles in circumference; formed like a funnel; and that it had in the middle a fpacious cavity. He afferted that he had made the circuit of it, along a kind of narrow ridge; that, from time to time, it threw out ftones and burning matters, to a confiderable height, roaring, and fhaking the ground; but that, in the intervals when it was undifturbed, he had obferved it without danger or difficulty.

In the time of Fazello, however, who vifited Etna after Cardinal Bembo, there were no longer two craters, but only one; the circumference of which, as he informs us, was four miles. It had the ufual form of the funnel, emitted fire and thick fmoke, but, at intervals, was calm, and might be approached;

approached; at which times a subterraneous noise was heard, and a sound like that of the boiling of an immense caldron on a vast fire. These observations were made by him in 1541, and 1554; in both which years the crater appears to have been single*.

These few citations appear to me sufficient to shew what changes have taken place in the summit of Etna, relative to the number, the form, and the size of its craters, according to the different effects of its conflagrations at different times. But there is likewise another alteration which should not be passed unnoticed, described by two writers who themselves observed it, Fazello and Borelli; I mean the falling in and absorption of the extreme summit of Etna within its crater. The former of the abovementioned authors relates that, in his time, there arose, in the mouth of the crater, a little hill, isolated on every side, which formed the vertex of the mountain; and

* Fazel. Sic.

which, in a terrible eruption, fell into, and was buried in, the gulf, thus enlarging the crater, and diminishing the height of the mountain. This hill itself had been produced by a former eruption in 1444*.

In like manner, Borelli informs us that, in the conflagration of 1669, the summit of Etna, which rose, like a tower, to a great height above the part which is level, was swallowed up in the deep gulf †.

I have already said, that, when I visited Etna, its summit was divided into two points, or little mountains, one of which rose a quarter of a mile above the other. I should not be surprised were I to hear that, in some new and fierce eruption, the highest of these had fallen in, and the two craters become one of much larger dimensions. We know that the summit of Vesuvius has sometimes fallen down in the same manner; nor

* Ubi sup.
† Ubi sup. See Plate I.

does it appear difficult to assign the cause. It seems to admit of no doubt that the highest parts of Etna, and other mountains which vomit fire from their summits, have their foundations on the sides of the crater, which extend to an immense depth. In any violent earthquake, therefore, or impetuous shock of the lava endeavouring to force a passage, it may easily be imagined that those foundations must be torn up and broken away, and the summit of the volcano fall and be lost in the gulf.

These dilapidations have not, however, from time immemorial, produced any sensible diminution of the height of the summit of Etna; since the losses occasioned by some eruptions are repaired by others which follow. This may be inferred from a phenomenon usually inseparable from the summit of Etna, though, by a rare accident, not observable at the time of my journey; I mean the ice and snow with which it is covered. Had any considerable decrease of the height of the mountain taken place, in

consequence

consequence of the summit repeatedly falling in, in former ages, the ice and snow would not, certainly, in a climate so mild, have continued to envelop the top of the mountain, as they now do, even during the greatest heats of summer. But this continual residence of the snow and ice on Etna has been celebrated by all antiquity; for near observation was not necessary to ascertain this phenomenon, since it is distinctly apparent at the distance of a hundred miles. " Adscendit ea regio (says Fazello, speaking of the Upper Region of Etna) passuum millia fere xii.; quæ per hyemem tota nivibus obsita extremisque frigoribus riget: per æstatem quoque nulla sui parte nec canitie nec gelu caret: quod equidem admiratione dignum est; cum vertex incendia prope sempiterna jugi flammarum eructatione inter nives ipsas pariat, enutriat, ac continuet.'

" This region extends nearly twelve miles;
" and, even in summer, is almost perpetually
" covered with snow, and extremely cold;
" which is the more wonderful as the sum-
" mit continually produces, nourishes, and
" pours

" pours forth flames, amid the ice and snow
" with which it is enveloped."

Solinus and Silius Italicus give the same description. The former says—" Mirum est quod in illa ferventis naturæ pervicacia mixtas ignibus (Ætna) nives profert: et licet vastis exundet incendiis, aprica canitie perpetuo brumalem detinet faciem *."
" Etna, in a wonderful manner, exhibits
" snows mixed with fires; and retains
" every appearance of the severest winter
" amid her vast conflagrations."

Silius Italicus has the following lines:

" Summo cana jugo cohibet (mirabile dictu)
Vicinam flammis glaciem, æternoque rigore
Ardentes horrent scopuli; stat vertice celsi
Collis hyems, calidaque nivem tegit atra favilla†."

" Where burning Etna, towering, threats the skies,
" 'Mid flames and ice the lofty rocks arise;
" The fire amid eternal winter glows,
" And the warm ashes hide the hoary snows."

And since I have quoted a poet, I will cite two others; Claudian and Pindar; as it

---

* Cap. xi.   † Lib. xiv.

is sufficiently evident that poetry here must express truth and not fiction.

" Sed quamvis nimio fervens exuberet æstu,
Scit nivibus fervare fidem : pariterque favillis
Durefcit glacies, tanti fecura vaporis,
Arcano defenfa gelu, fumoque fideli
Lambit contiguas innoxia flamma pruinas *."

" Amid the fires accumulates the fnow,
" And froft remains where burning afhes glow ;
" O'er ice eternal fweep th' inactive flames,
" And winter, fpite of fire, the region claims."

Thus the Latin poet ; but the Greek has given us a picture of Etna much more highly coloured, reprefenting it not only as the eternal abode of fnows, but as the column of heaven, to exprefs its aftonifhing height.

" Κιων δ' ερανια
Νιφοεσσ' Αίτνα παντες
Χιονες οξειας τιθηνα †."

—" Snowy Etna, nurfe of endlefs froft,
" The mighty prop of heaven."

---

* Claud. de Rapt. Prof.
† Pind. Pyth. Od. i.

It is to be remarked that Pindar lived five hundred years before the Christian æra.

I now return from this digression, which, though not, indeed, very short, appears to me perfectly appropriate to the subject; and proceed to resume my narrative. I shall first speak briefly of a phenomenon relative to the smoke which arises from the crater of Etna, and which was seen differently by Mr. Brydone, Count Borch, and myself. Mr. Brydone tells us that " from " many places of the crater issue volumes " of sulphureous smoke, which being much " heavier than the circumambient air, in- " stead of rising in it, as smoke generally " does, immediately on its getting out of " the crater, rolls down the side of the moun- " tain, like a torrent, till coming to that " part of the atmosphere of the same spe- " cific gravity with itself, it shoots off hori- " zontally, and forms a large track in the " air according to the direction of the " wind."

On the contrary, the smoke when seen by Count Borch, at the intervals when the air was calm, arose, perpendicularly, to a great height, and afterwards fell, like white fleeces, on the top of the mountain. I shall not presume to doubt these two facts, though I observed neither of them. The two columns of smoke which I saw, though bent somewhat from the perpendicular by the wind, ascended with the usual promptitude of ordinary smoke (a certain proof that it was considerably lighter than the ambient air), and, when at a great height, became extremely rarefied and dispersed. This difference in the appearance of the smoke, as observed by the two authors before mentioned and myself, may arise not only from the gravity of the air on Etna being different at different times, but also from the diversity of the smoke, which may be sometimes lighter and sometimes heavier than the air that surrounds it; differing in its nature according to the quality of the substances from which it is produced. Such a variation in its specific gravity must induce us to conclude

conclude that the bodies which burn within the crater are specifically different.

The effects of the air at the summit of Etna, as experienced by myself and some of the travellers I have before cited, were, likewise, different. Sir William Hamilton tells us, that the thinness of that fluid occasioned a difficulty of respiration; and Count Borch appears to have experienced a still greater inconvenience of that kind, since he says—" The rarity of the air on this moun-
" tain is extremely sensible, and almost ren-
" ders that fluid unfit for respiration." On the contrary, Baron Riedesel felt no such effect, as far, at least, as we can judge from his own words. " I did not perceive, as
" several travellers have asserted, that the
" air here is so thin and rarefied as to pre-
" vent, or at least greatly incommode, respi-
" ration." Mr. Brydone has said nothing on the subject, and his silence may induce us to conclude that he experienced no difficulty.

I, my

I, my servant, and the two guides, suffered no inconvenience from the air. The exertions we had made, indeed, in climbing up the craggy steep declivities which surround the crater, had produced a shortness of breathing; but when we had reached the summit, and recovered from our weariness by rest, we felt no kind of inconvenience, either while sitting, or when, incited by curiosity, we went round and examined different parts of the edges of the crater. The same is affirmed by Borelli: " Æquè bene respiratio in cacumine Ætnæ absolvitur, ac in locis subjectis campestribus."— " Respiration is performed with the same " ease on the top of Etna, as in the country " below."

Several writers have treated of the difficulty of respiration experienced by those who travel over high mountains, and other inconveniencies to which they are exposed; but none, in my opinion, more judiciously than M. Saussure, in his Travels among the Alps. The observations he has made appear

pear to me to explain the cauſe of theſe different accounts, relative to the effect of the air on the top of Etna. When the height above the level of the ſea was 2450 poles, or nearly ſuch, which he found to be that of Mount Blanc, every individual felt more or leſs inconvenience from the rarefaction of the air, as happened to himſelf and nineteen perſons who accompanied him, when, in Auguſt 1787, he aſcended that mountain. But when the elevation was much leſs, as for example, 1900 poles, ſome of theſe perſons felt no difficulty, among whom was this naturaliſt; though he confeſſes that he began to experience inconvenience as he aſcended higher. We have not indeed any certain obſervations relative to the exact height of Etna, as is ſufficiently proved by the different eſtimates given by different naturaliſts. Signor Dangios, however, aſtronomer at Malta, in the year 1787, meaſured the height of this mountain by a geometrical method, and the public anxiouſly expects the reſults, which will ſatisfactorily ſolve this important problem. In the mean time, from comparing

the

the measures hitherto assigned, the elevation of Etna above the level of the sea is probably somewhat less than 1900 poles. Hence we understand why respiration, in many persons, is not incommoded, while the contrary happens to others, according to the different strength and habit of body of different individuals.

After having, for two hours, indulged my eyes with a view of the interior of the crater, that is, in the contemplation of a spectacle which, in its kind, and in the present age, is without a parallel in the world; I turned them to another scene, which is likewise unequalled for the multiplicity, the beauty and the variety of the objects it presents. In fact, there is, perhaps, no elevated region on the whole globe which offers, at one view, so ample an extent of sea and land as the summit of Etna. The first of the sublime objects which it presents is the immense mass of its own colossal body. When in the country below it, near Catania, we raise our eyes to this sovereign of the mountains, we
$\hspace{10em}$ certainly

certainly survey it with admiration, as it rises majestically, and lifts its lofty head above the clouds; and with a kind of geometric glance we estimate its height from the base to the summit: but we only see it in profile. Very different is the appearance it presents, viewed from its towering top, when the whole of its enormous bulk is subjected to the eye. The first part, and that nearest the observer, is the Upper Region, which, from the quantity of snows and ice beneath which it is buried during the greater part of the year, may be called the frigid zone, but which, at that time, was divested of this covering, and only exhibited rough and craggy cliffs, here piled on each other, and there separate, and rising perpendicularly; fearful to view and impossible to ascend. Towards the middle of this zone, an assemblage of fugitive clouds, irradiated by the sun, and all in motion, increased the wild variety of the scene. Lower down, appeared the Middle Region, which, from the mildness of its climate, may merit the name of the temperate zone. Its numerous woods,

woods, interrupted in various places, seem, like a torn garment, to discover the nudity of the mountain. Here arise a multitude of other mountains, which in any other situation would appear of gigantic size, but are but pigmies compared to Etna. These have all originated from fiery eruptions. Lastly, the eye contemplates, with admiration, the Lower Region, which, from its violent heat, may claim the appellation of the torrid zone; the most extensive of the three, adorned with elegant villas and castles, verdant hills, and flowery fields, and terminated by the extensive coast, where, to the south, stands the beautiful city of Catania, to which the waves of the neighbouring sea serve as a mirror.

But not only do we discover, from this astonishing elevation, the entire massy body of Mount Etna; but the whole of the island of Sicily, with all its noble cities, lofty hills, extensive plains, and meandering rivers. In the indistinct distance we perceive Malta; but have a clear view of the environs of
Messina,

Meffina, and the greater part of Calabria; while Lipari, the fuming Vulcano, the blazing Stromboli, and the other Eolian ifles, appear immediately under our feet, and feem as if, on ftooping down, we might touch them with the finger.

Another object no lefs fuperb and majeftic, was the far-ftretching furface of the fubjacent fea which furrounded me, and led my eye to an immenfe diftance, till it feemed gradually to mingle with the heavens.

Seated in the midft of this theatre of the wonders of Nature, I felt an indefcribable pleafure from the multiplicity and beauty of the objects I furveyed; and a kind of internal fatisfaction and exultation of heart. The fun was advancing to the meridian, unobfcured by the fmalleft cloud, and Reaumur's thermometer ftood at the tenth degree above the freezing point. I was therefore in that temperature which is moft friendly to man; and the refined air I breathed, as

if

if it had been entirely vital, communicated a vigour and agility to my limbs, and an activity and life to my ideas, which appeared to be of a celestial nature.

Not without regret, I, at length, recollected it was time to return, and relinquish this enchanting scene; since I had determined to pass the ensuing night at San Niccolo dell' Arena, to avoid the hard bed and inconveniencies of the Grotto delle Capre. I had resolved, likewise, to return to Catania by another way, in order to examine objects which might render my journey of greater utility. The road I took, the objects which presented themselves, and the observations I made on them, I shall relate in the following chapter.

CHAP. IX.

RETURN FROM MOUNT ETNA TO CATANIA.

Manner in which the Author descended with ease and security from the summit of Etna—Materials of which the Torre del Filosofo is composed—Confirmation that the lava which flowed in October 1787, is still internally penetrated by the fire—The observation that the secondary mountains on the sides of Etna are of volcanic origin, not novel but antient—Probability that Monte Rosso was the result of a partial eruption which had no communication with the crater of Etna—Another eruption from the sides of Etna which had no connection with that crater—Great want of water experienced by the peasants who inhabit Etna, from a long dry season—Affecting incident arising from this circumstance—A scarcity of springs common in volcanized countries—
The

The Scogli de' Ciclopi, or Rocks of the Cyclops—Some of them, but not all, of a prismatic conformation—Zeolites found on these rocks—Vitrification of those zeolites in the furnace—Pumices not found on Mount Etna, as has been affirmed by Count Borch, and others—Animals observed by the Author in the Middle and Upper Regions of Etna—Two Museums in Catania already known to strangers, and a third lately established, valuable for its contents—Natural History little cultivated at Catania, with respect to that part which relates to the Mineral Kingdom; but more relatively to the Animal.

THE ascent up the steep and craggy cone of Etna, though not more than a mile in a direct line, cost me, as I have already said, three hours of laborious and fatiguing exertion. It seems scarcely necessary to say that the descent employed me less time, but the difference greatly exceeded my expectation. I found that to effect this descent nothing

thing more was required, but to fix my feet firmly on some large piece of scoria, and balance my body, since that piece, from almost the smallest impulse I could give it, would slide swiftly down the descent, and convey me to a considerable distance, till stopped by the accumulation of the lesser pieces of scoriæ which it drove before it; when I had only to select another large piece, on which I again glided down as before; only taking care, with the staff I held in my hand, to turn aside the pieces of scoriæ which followed me in my descent, that they might not strike against and wound my legs. In this manner, in a few minutes, I arrived at the bottom of that declivity.

A little below the summit of Etna, are the ruins of a very ancient fabric, called La Torre del Filosofo, the Tower of the Philosopher; it having been pretended, and believed by many, that it was built by Empedocles, that he might fix his habitation in a place convenient for observing the conflagrations of Etna. Others imagine it to have

been

been an ancient temple of some deity; while others have conjectured that it was a watch-tower, built by the Normans, to observe the motions of their enemies, and give notice of them, by some signal, to the different bodies of troops scattered over the island. It is very apparent that these, and other opinions which I omit for the sake of brevity, are very inconclusive with respect to the real use and design of this ruined edifice, which could but little attract the notice of history. I did not visit it in my journey to Etna, having been conducted another way by my guides. Nor should I have regretted not having seen it, had I not reflected, that the great antiquity of the fabric might justly excite a curiosity to examine the materials, and ascertain whether they were lateritious or volcanic. This induced me, after I had returned to Italy, to write to the Abbate Francesco Ferrara, at Catania, a person well versed in the science of nature, requesting him to send me, to Pavia, some specimens of the materials of which the Torre del Filosofo was composed. He very politely complied

complied with my requeft, and I found, on examination, that thefe materials were of the following kind. They confift, firft, of a cement of lime, which, by length of time, has become carbonate of lime; in which cement were incorporated great numbers of pieces of black cellular fcoriæ of lava; but fo changed by the effect of time, that many of them were become externally pulverulent, and internally extremely friable. The fhoerls they contained had likewife loft, at the fuperfices of the fcoriæ, their natural lineaments, and all their luftre, and were become fo foft that they might every where be cut with the point of a penknife. This cement was, in the fecond place, united to two kinds of lava, which exhaled an argillaceous odour in their fractures, and had for their bafe the hornftone. One of thefe was very compact, extremely hard, of a ferruginous colour, a fine grain, with numerous feltfpar points fcattered in it. The other was a grey colour, of rather a fine texture, and contained an incredible quantity of feltfpars; fo that, when viewed with a lens, by the clear light

light of the fun, it appeared extremely brilliant. The materials, therefore, of this edifice, whatever was its original deftination, were, in part, taken from the place, with the addition of a cement of lime, to give the building the neceffary folidity *.

I, afterwards, again croffed the lava which flowed in October 1787, and, as I returned by a different way, I found myfelf near another part of it, where it ftill remained extremely hot; which tended to confirm me in my opinion that the internal and central part of this lava ftill contains a very active and ftrong fire.

Having reached the middle region, I afcended fome of thofe mountains which I had obferved from the fummit of Etna, and which, from their conical figure, and the ca-

* I have read, in the works of fome travellers, that fragments of brick and marble are found in the Torre del Filofofo; but the Abbate Ferrara has affured me that fuch fragments no longer exift.

vity at their top, clearly shew that they are the productions of fire *. I was, in fact, convinced that they bear unequivocal marks of the effects of that destructive agent, in an accumulation of lavas, scoriæ, and volcanic sand.

Another

---

* I had at first believed that the observation that these mountains are truly volcanic was of late date, referring it to Sir William Hamilton, who has described their conical form, and the crater, or incavation at their summit; but I find it to be very old, since it is mentioned by Borelli, and, before him, by Fazello. The following are the words of the former: " Extant nè-
" dum in summitate Ætnæ, sed etiam in ejus dorso,
" campestres voragines, quæ habent fere omnes peculi-
" arem monticulam adinstar verrucæ in animalis cute
" exporrectæ; suntque prædicti colles valde acclives,
" habentque figuram coni acutanguli plano parallelo
" basi dissecti; et in summitate cujuslibet eorum sinuosa
" cavitas reperitur, a qua olim flammæ, arenæ, et
" glaræ exierunt."—" Extinct vortices (or craters)
" are found not only on the summit of Etna, but also
" on the sides. They have almost all of them their
" peculiar hills, projecting like a wart on the skin of
" an animal; which hills are extremely steep, and
" have the figure of a rectangular cone dissected pa-
" rallel to its base. At the top of each is a sinuous ca-
" vity,

Another enquiry relative to these mountains here naturally suggests itself. Is their origin derived from the melted matter contained within the immense abyss of Etna, which, unable to reach the crater, from the excessive height, has burst forth through its sides, and thus formed these mountains? or, as is perhaps more probable, have they been produced by particular conflagrations and eruptions which have no communication with the immense furnace within the crater?

"vity, from which formerly issued flames, sand, and "lava."

We know that by *glarea* he means lava; in fact, at Catania, it is still called *sciara*.

Fazello had before observed and described these volcanic hills. His words are: "Plurimos præterea nemo "rosos et editos offendimus colles, quorum cacumina "voragines, licet silvescentes, exhibebant. Eos veterem "esse materiam ex visceribus montis olim proditam, "postremi profluvii hiatus, qui similem fere formam, "enatasque recens habet arbores, arguebat."—"We "likewise find several lofty hills, the tops of which, "though overgrown with wood, exhibit the appearance "of craters. The mouth of the last eruption, which "is nearly of the same form, and already bears trees, "renders it probable that they are composed of the

"matter

crater? I know that the generality of volcanists embrace the former opinion, and reject the latter with contempt; and I find, that, whenever the lesser mountains are produced on the sides of the principal volcano, by the means of eruptions, they usually have recourse to this hypothesis for the explication of the cause. Thus, since the eruptions of lava which have issued from the crater of Vesuvius are much more numerous than those of Etna, they endeavour to account for the

" matter anciently ejected from the bowels of the
" mountain."

The same observation is likewise repeated by D'Orville, who, in 1727, visited Etna—" Colles hi non so-
" lum circum magnum craterem (Ætnæ), verum etiam
" inde per circuitum viginti mille passuum et ultra in
" toto monte disperfi sunt. Omnes hos colles aliquan-
" do igneam materiam e summo vertice ejecisse, om-
" nia suadent; et in multis hujus rei adeo aperta extant
" vestigia, ut nemo dubitare possit. Quin ipse in cul-
" mine collis illius, quem *metæ* similem diximus, positos
" in verticibus nonnullorum crateres depressos, et plane
" undique lapidum exustorum congerie circundatos
" animadverti."—" These hills are not only found ad-
" joining to the great crater, but are dispersed in a cir-
" cuit of twenty miles and more, and, indeed, through-
" out

the difference, by alleging, that, in confequence of the fmall height of the former volcano, the lava can more eafily reach the crater; whereas, in the latter, it is compelled to force a paffage through the fide, from being unable to rife to fo prodigious an elevation.

I readily admit, that this frequently happens; but inftances may certainly be cited which afford ftrong reafons to believe that the production of the lateral mountain arifes from partial eruptions, which have no communication with the principal crater. Of this Monte Roffo is an example. In the

"out the whole mountain. Every appearance proves
"that all thefe hills have once ejected a fiery matter
"from their fummits; and in many the traces of this
"are fo evident, that it is impoffible to entertain a doubt.
"The remains of craters are apparent, and they are
"frequently furrounded with accumulations of burnt
"ftones."

Thus we find the defcription given by the Englifh naturalift of this leffer volcanic mountain, had been preceded by that of a Sicilian, an Italian, and a Dutch writer, all eye-witneffes of what they defcribed.

morning of the 11th of March 1669, a vast cleft opened not far from the place in which, afterwards, Monte Rosso arose, and extended for the space of ten miles, in the direction of the grand crater of Etna, (V. V. V. Plate I.) On the night following, in the place where this mountain now stands, another large cleft opened, from which were immediately ejected immense clouds of smoke, and showers of melted stones, preceded by a tremendous noise, and violent concussions of the earth.

On the night of the 12th, a river of lava poured down; and, the next day, a prodigious quantity of sand and stones was thrown out. Yet, during all these subterranean thunders, convulsions of the earth, streams of lava, and showers of stones, the upper crater of Etna was perfectly undisturbed, and only, from time to time, emitted some light smoke which had before issued, and is usual in its greatest state of tranquillity*. I know not whether I am mistaken in considering this

* Borelli, ubi sup.

as a probable proof that there is no communication between the higheft mouth of Etna, and the new one which has opened in the fide fome miles diftant from it. I have obferved likewife, with Borelli, that the higheft crater, having remained filent and at reft until the twenty-fifth day, afterwards began to rage with the fame fymptoms of fmoke, thunders, earthquakes, and ejected fand and ftones; and in fine, by the ruin of its fummit, precipitated and buried in its gulph. It feems extremely probable, that this change has been effected by the breaking away of the ftony mafs which feparated the old and new gulphs, in confequence of which the fire and effervefcent matters forced their paffage, and difcharged themfelves from another opening at the fummit of the mountain.

We muft not omit to notice another fact related by the fame writer, which, though it does not refpect the formation of any mountain on the fides of Etna, independent of a communication with its higheft crater, may

may authorize us to conclude, that some lateral gulph may open and disgorge fiery torrents without any such communication. Such an eruption happened in 1636, when the ground, nine miles from the summit of Etna, opened in two places, and poured out two torrents of lava without any appearance of fire or smoke at the summit of the mountain. It is very probable that we should have accounts of other similar eruptions, and other mountains formed on the sides of Etna, had the ancients studied and recorded the conflagrations of that mountain, in the manner the moderns have begun to observe and describe them.

Whatever may be the matters which cause and continue volcanos, it is only necessary that they should exist and take fire in a place that has no communication with the central volcano, to produce partial eruptions and mountains, which may very naturally be supposed to happen.

After having slept at San Niccolo dell Arena

Arena the night preceding the 5th of September, I set out early the next morning, taking my way by the *Rocks of the Cyclops*, celebrated for the basaltiform lavas of which they consist. In this part of my journey I continually passed over lavas, and through several villages built upon them.

A short time before I reached the rocks I was in search of, a scene presented itself, which, though foreign to my subject, the sentiment of humanity and compassion we feel on witnessing the misfortunes of our fellow-creatures will not permit me to pass in silence.

Mount Etna has at all times been very deficient in springs; but when I was there the scarcity of water was extreme, not a drop of rain having fallen for nine months; and the rain-water which the peasants of these places had collected in cisterns being exhausted, they were obliged to go in search of it to those parts of the mountain where a scanty spring might still be found. Though

in

In my journey up Etna I had sufficient reason to notice this scarcity of water, by being made to pay for it much dearer than for wine at Catania, I was much more convinced of it when, on my way, I saw a number of women and girls carrying barrels on beasts of burden, to fill with water at a spring on one side of the road. But the scene which made the greatest impression on me, I met with on my return, in the vicinity of Jaci; where I saw more than a hundred poor mountaineers of both sexes, who had come thither to quench their thirst at a stream of water which issued from the midst of the lava. It strongly excited my pity to see these wretched peasants, all bare-footed, exposed to a burning sun, for the heat was then very great in those low parts of the mountain; and labouring and sweating under the load of large earthen vessels, which they had brought on their shoulders and heads, a distance of more than ten miles, to carry home water. When they came within sight of the spring, they exerted all the strength they retained, hastened their weary steps, and, when they reached it, began to drink with extreme eagerness, without for a long time taking away their lips. How much was my commiseration increased, when they informed me they were obliged to perform this laborious journey every day, that is, to employ the whole day in it; travelling from the time of sun-rise till noon to reach the spring, and from noon to the dusk of the evening to regain their habitations, and carry refreshment to their parched families! While I was listening to their sad story, it chanced that one of them, a boy about thirteen years of age, in setting down the vessel he carried on his shoulder, let it slip, I know not how, out of his hand, and it broke by the fall. Words can scarcely describe the consternation, grief, and anguish, with which he appeared transfixed at the accident, while with bitter tears and in broken exclamations he lamented his misfortune, and expressed his fears of the consequences he apprehended to myself, from his being thus disabled from carrying home to his thirsty parents

rents the expected supply. As little is it possible to describe the joy, delight, and lively sentiment of gratitude which he expressed, on my giving him a small piece of money, that he might buy, in a neighbouring village, another vessel to replace that which was broken, and complete with the usual success his laborious journey.

Etna is not alone scantily supplied with springs. I have observed a similar scarcity of them in the Eolian or Lipari islands, as we shall see in another part of this work; and if I am not mistaken, the same want of them will be found in other volcanic countries; the cause of which appears to me evident. The rains which descend on mountains of this kind, either fall on bibacious tufas or scoriaceous matters, in which they sink deep without again appearing on the surface in the lower places, because they meet with no argillaceous or stony strata to detain them; whereas such strata are frequent in mountains not volcanic, and produce numerous

merous dropping springs, fountains, and sources of rivers, as we find in the Alps and Apennines.

When again the rains fall on the solid and compact lavas, they do not sink into them, but run down their declivities, forming indeed rivers and torrents, in the rainy season, but never true springs. In several parts of Etna, and especially near the Grotta delle Capre, I have seen large furrows hollowed in the lavas, by the continued action of the rain-water.

Two hours after noon I arrived at the rocks of the Cyclops; which are likewise termed islands because surrounded by the sea, though they are scarcely a stone's throw from the shore on which the village of Trezza stands. It is possible that they might once make a part of the sides of Etna, and have been separated from them by the sea; or they may have been thrown up out of the water by partial eruptions. I examined them, first making the circuit of them in a boat, and then afcending them to obferve their parts.

It is immediately apparent that fome of thefe rocks confift externally only of prifmatic columns, which fall perpendicularly into the fea, in fome places of the length of one foot, in others two, and in others more; but it is certain that other parts of thefe rocks have not the leaft prifmatic appearance, and are only full of very irregular fiffures, which have divided them into irregular pieces, as we frequently fee in common lavas.

The rocks of the Cyclops prefent another object which has not efcaped the acute examination of M. Dolomieu; I mean the numerous and various zeolites of great beauty which are found on their furface, and even in the middle of their fubftance, where there are fmall pores and cavities. That naturalift thinks, with great reafon, that thefe noble ftones, after the congelation of the lavas, derived their origin from the waters which filtrated through them, and held in folution

tion the particles proper for the production of zeolites. It would be a useless labour were I to attempt their description after it has been so well given by M. Dolomieu; I shall, therefore, only mention what I observed in them when I examined them in the furnace.

If we take small pieces of lava, detached from the rocks to which the zeolites adhere, leave them for some time in the fire, and observe them after they have cooled, the following are the results:

The zeolites, though the lava, their matrix, has not undergone a complete fusion, are vitrified, and have flowed over the surface of the lava, forming a leaf of glass; but the greater part become globules, which, from their lucid milky whiteness, resemble pearls. When examined with the lens, these globules are found to be full of cracks, probably caused by the sudden removal of the lavas from the furnace into the cold air. This glass is semitransparent and hard.

If we break the pieces of lava expofed to the fire and examine the fractures, we fhall find that only a femivitrification has taken place in the zeolites they contain. Some of thefe zeolitic lavas are of a homogeneous fubftance, but others include fmall fhoerls. The magnet attracts the powder of them, and fome have polarity, attracting one end of the magnetic needle, and repelling the other.

I have but a few obfervations more to make, relative to Etna. Count Borch, not perfectly fatisfied with the received divifion of the mountain into three Regions, the lower, the middle, and the higher, has added a fourth, which he calls the region of fnow; and each of the four regions he again fub-divides into feveral diftricts. I fhall not difpute with him thefe minute diftinctions, which, whether they tend more to clearnefs or confufion may be difficult to determine. I fhall only make fome brief remarks on his diftrict of fcoriæ, in the fecond region, of which he fays: " The diftrict of fcoriæ contains a
" furface

"surface of two miles entirely covered with "pumices, ashes, and scoriæ."

Without noticing the scoriæ and ashes, I know not what he understood by *pumices*. The truth is, that Etna affords none; as Dolomieu, who so minutely examined the mountain, has expresly asserted; and, as I took nearly the same road with Borch, I must have met with them had they been so plentiful as he describes. The Chevalier Gioeni, likewise, in his account of the products of the eruption of 1787, describing one which, in its configuration, resembles the porous pumices of Lipari, remarks that this is the first time that Etna has ejected such a kind of stone [*].

In

---

[*] Borch is not the only person who has fallen into this error. Sir William Hamilton, when he visited Etna, found there no pumices; but he was told by the Canon Recupero of Catania that the mountain produced them: the Canon, however, it is well known, was unacquainted with the first principles of lithology. Baron Riedesel, who, in this part of science, was, perhaps, not superior to the Canon, says that pumice is among the number of stones ejected by Etna; and joins with it

In my journey to Etna, and on my return, at the same time that I examined volcanic objects I did not neglect to observe whether the two more elevated regions of the mountain were inhabited by animals. A little beyond Monte Rosso, I bought five partridges *(Tetrao rufus Lin.)* of a sportsman who had shot them at the upper extremity of the middle region. These I had roasted at San Niccolo dell' Arena, and they furnished me with two good meals. In crossing the same region I met with several birds of the titmouse species *(Parus major; Parus cæruleus Lin.)*, a kite *(Falco milvus)*, thee jays *(Corvus glandularius)*, two thrushes *(Turdus viscivorus)*; and several ravens and crows *(Corvus corax; Corvus corone)*:

the sand-stone; a production which, according to those best acquainted with the mineralogy of volcanos, is as much a stranger to Etna as the pumice. One of these writers may, probably, have induced M. Sage to assert that " Etna throws out a great quantity of pumices." This gross error was probably occasioned by the resemblance which, to persons little acquainted with such substances, scoriæ and cellular lavas appear to have to pumices.

half

half way up the higher region I saw no other animals, except some lion-ants *(Myrmeleon formicarum Linn.)* which made their pit-falls in the dust of the lavas. There were several of them in a dusty corner of the Grotta delle Capre. As they live by ensnaring other small animals, and especially ants, in the slippery pits they form; it may be necessary to observe, that these are not wanting there, though I did not see them.

The city of Catania, during my stay there, amply afforded me the means of amusement and instruction. The two Museums, the one belonging to the Prince di Biscari, and the other to the Benedictine Fathers, besides the various objects they contain relative to the arts and antiquities, are also furnished with a collection of natural productions, and will be found to correspond to the great expectations that may have been formed of them from the advantageous descriptions of Riedesel, Brydone, and Borch. That of the Prince is distinguished by some rare specimens which might adorn the richest and moſt extenſive collections. But in that city a third muſeum, hitherto little known, becauſe it is new, is beginning to flouriſh. It may be ſaid it is yet in its infancy; but the infant may become a giant. The poſſeſſor and founder of it is the Chevalier Gioeni. His firſt intention was to collect the moſt curious and intereſting productions of the Sicilian ſea; and he has ſucceeded admirably. We here find dry preparations of the fiſhes moſt remarkable for their form or the rarity of their ſpecies. Among the numerous families of zoophyta, the alcyonia, the antipathes, the cellulariæ, the eſcharæ, the pennatulæ, the ſertulariæ, the milleporæ, and the iſides (corals), are not wanting; but the madreporæ and the gorgonæ are the moſt conſpicuous for their beauty and rarity. It is equally well furniſhed with ſpecimens of the principal cruſtaceous animals of that ſea, but the numerous and choſen collection of thoſe of the teſtaceous kind is the principal ornament of the Muſeum. With reſpect to theſe, we find a practice adopted we meet with in no other cabinet. As

there

there are some extremely minute shells, in size not exceeding a grain of sand, which it is impossible to view distinctly with the naked eye, they are as it were lost in the greater part of other Museums; but here they are placed, methodically distributed, at the bottom of small tubes, at the other end of which is a lens; by the aid of which, the eye is enabled to discover the beauty of the colours, the peculiarity of the involutions, the infinite variety of the forms, the windings of the apertures, the cavities, prominences, points, threads, &c. In fine, these points of organized matter, by this means, equally with the larger crustaceous animals, afford pleasure to the eyes of the curious, and useful instruction to the learned, for characterizing the species.

The Chevalier Gioeni, in consequence of his researches relative to these aquatic animals, has distinguished himself by the discovery of a new genus of multivalve conchylia, which he has already made known; but he will do himself much more honour by by the publication of a work on the subject on which he is now employed.

He has not confined himself to marine productions, but has extended his diligence to terrestrial; and the neighbouring volcano has added to his collection. We here find specimens of all the Etnean products; and amid the multitude of various lavas he has collected, he has discovered a new species, which he has denominated *fibrous*. The method he has adopted of placing the different lavas with the stones and primitive rocks, from which they derive their origin, is highly instructive.

Equally conducive to the advancement of knowledge is the numerous series of testaceous fossils, which he has collected with great labour, to the north-east of Etna, in a situation more than three hundred poles above the level of the sea. These extremely resemble the natural which are now found in the neighbouring waters. But as the time when the sea reached to that height is certainly anterior

anterior to the annals of hiſtory, of what great antiquity muſt the volcano be which exiſted before that epocha!

The productions of this part of Sicily are accompanied with thoſe of the reſt of the iſland. We find a noble collection of marbles and jaſpers, with various minerals, and cryſtallized ſulphurs.

Though this Muſeum deſerves great commendation for the multiplicity and choice of the objects collected within a few years, it perhaps deſerves ſtill greater praiſe for the accurate and judicious manner in which every part of it is ſyſtematiſed; a regulation extremely neceſſary in every collection, and which it is to be wiſhed might be introduced into the two other Muſeums before mentioned.

I have been ſomewhat more diffuſe in my deſcription of this collection, becauſe it merited to be known to foreigners, who, ſhould they chance to viſit Catania, may, by its means,

means, procure information of various productions of Sicily and the neighbouring sea, which they might elsewhere seek in vain.

The Chevalier Gioeni is Professor of Natural History in the university of his country, which can likewise boast of other men of genius, principally in polite literature. The natural sciences, especially those which have relation to the fossil kingdom, are not the most cultivated; less I believe from indisposition towards them, than from want of encouragement. It is not the same with respect to the other two kingdoms. While I was at Catania, I had the honour to receive visits from several persons of learning; and I found that more than one of them had read with advantage the works of Bonnet, Buffon, and Duhamel. Among them may be distinguished the Abbate Don Francesco Ferrara, who afforded me the opportunity of examining the materials of the Torre del Filosofo. The taste for these extensive branches of natural history must become greater, and spread more extensively,

from

from the laudable example set by Signor ⸺ Ferrara, who has lately published in Sicily, *The Contemplation of Nature* of the philosopher of Geneva (Bonnet): to which he has added, besides my notes and those of others, a great number of his own, replete with learning and good sense, which must render such a work still more valuable.

END OF THE FIRST VOLUME.

The Summit of Mount Etna.

www.ingramcontent.com/pod-product-compliance
Lightning Source LLC
Chambersburg PA
CBHW032043220426
43664CB00008B/831